A Relevant Way to Read

A Relevant Way to Read

A New Approach to Exegesis and Communication

Margaret G. Sim

PICKWICK *Publications* • Eugene, Oregon

A RELEVANT WAY TO READ
A New Approach to Exegesis and Communication

Pickwick Publications
An Imprint of Wipf and Stock Publishers
199 W. 8th Ave., Suite 3
Eugene, OR 97401

www.wipfandstock.com

PAPERBACK ISBN: 978-1-5326-0367-9
HARDCOVER ISBN: 978-1-5326-0368-6

Cataloging-in-Publication data:

Names: Sim, Margaret G.

Title: A relevant way to read : a new approach to exegesis and communication / Margaret G. Sim.

Description: Eugene, OR: Pickwick Publications, 2016. | Includes bibliographical references and index.

Identifiers: ISBN 978-1-5326-0367-9 (paperback) | ISBN 978-1-5326-0368-6 (hardcover)

Subjects: LCSH: Bible. New Testament—Criticism, interpretation, etc. | Bible. New Testament—Hermeneutics. | Bible. Gospels—Criticism, interpretation, etc. | Bible. Gospels—Hermeneutics. | Bible. Epistles of Paul—Criticism, interpretation, etc. | Bible. Epistles of Paul—Hermeneutics.

Classification: BS2361.3 S5627 2016 (print)

Manufactured in the U.S.A. JULY 6, 2016

Contents

Chapter 1
Introduction

'Communication' has become a buzz word in recent years. Lack of communication is said to be the cause of so many of our present-day ills, from the breakdown of relationships to arrogant politicians, and poor service on every level. Humans seem to be passionate about knowing the latest information, while retaining the right to keep to themselves personal material. How we *interpret* communication is seldom considered. If we think about it at all, we might assume that words have meanings and we all understand these meanings – rather like a code which can be mechanically deciphered.

In fact, human communication is considerably more complex than this, and yet at the same time more transparent. Although words do convey meaning, we use context and encyclopaedic knowledge to make inferences from these words, and enrich the communication. In the physical world, humans begin to infer as soon as they see another human, before verbal communication has even begun. Indeed, humans seem to be incapable of desisting from inferencing. This description of how we communicate will be examined in detail in Chapter Two, but first of all we must accept that a new approach to the way in which we view language is worth the effort, particularly for biblical scholars.

Although many of the examples given in these chapters may appear to be concerned with oral communication only, I will show that the way of communication being explained relates well to literary texts, too, and in particular to biblical texts. Different genres of text are included and I invite you to consider the proposition that literalness in a text is not privileged. It is not the default option!

The approach I am taking has been compared with the fairly recent concern about the deconstruction of texts. This has sometimes given the impression that there are *no* meanings in a text. It would be more accurate to say that we cannot limit the meanings of a text. Even a committed deconstructionist such as Derrida wrote and published a considerable number of books, which would not have been the case if he did not believe that there would be readers who would derive some meaning from his writings. I do not undervalue the contribution that a deconstructionist approach brings to interpretation, but the early responses seemed to display deep pessimism about the whole interpretive exercise.

> Deconstruction reveals above all that no reading, whether of the author, the original reader or later interpreter, has the right to a final word about a text's meaning.[1]

I would suggest then that the very fact of creating a text for public view implies that the writer has an interest in making something manifest to someone other than himself.[2] He is indicating his intention to communicate. This may seem trite, but it is a necessary presupposition to any attempt to interpret an utterance.[3] If a writer has the intention to communicate, then the effort of interpretation is not a futile one. It may not be successful, but it is certainly worth the effort. Authorial intention has been regarded as an irrecoverable notion in recent scholarship, but given the communicator's 'intention to inform' it is a legitimate exercise to attempt to find clues to such intention in the speech or text, even if there is no certainty. The approach I explain in these chapters, in contrast to a deconstructionist approach, has more explanatory power to interpret not only how we communicate, but also how such communication may fail.

Alison Jack comments usefully on this lack of certainty in interpretation:

1. Jack, A. (1999) *Texts Reading Texts, Sacred and Secular.* JSNT 179. Sheffield: Sheffield Academic Press, p. 207.
2. The speaker or writer will be referred to as 'he', and the hearer or reader as 'she'.
3. Clark, B. (2013) *Relevance Theory.* Cambridge: CUP, p. 117. 'Any piece of writing makes mutually manifest that the communicator has an intention to inform.'

> Before the rise of 'historical anxiety' (p. 283) in the eighteenth century, reading of the Bible was characterized by a flexibility of interpretation which shares features both with midrash and deconstruction.[1]

Earlier readers of biblical texts were more innovative in their interpretive methods and less concerned with 'authorial intent'. The biblical text has been read and commented on for more than 2,000 years, and so it is important to have a sense of perspective in our interpretation, particularly in the context of our modern assumptions concerning accuracy. In relation to midrash, the former Chief Rabbi Jonathan Sacks regularly points out that Jewish exegesis involves Scripture dialoguing with Scripture, and also with life. As new situations arise, and a larger canvas is displayed, Jews are compelled to go back to the Torah and seek new insights.

> The *interpretation* of this text (Torah) has been the subject of an ongoing conversation for as long as Jews have studied the divine word, a conversation that began with Sinai thirty-three centuries ago and has not ceased since. Every age has added its commentaries, and so must ours.[2]

The Church Fathers also display a more innovative approach to their interaction with Scripture, and while we may not agree with their interpretation, we do need to exercise some humility in our perceived hermeneutical superiority. In attempting to interpret written text – and of course oral communication – we have to acknowledge that thoughts are private and only language is public. Comments such as 'I say what I think' or 'thinking out loud' may suggest that such thoughts are recoverable from the sounds uttered, but what we recover is a resemblance to or representation of such thoughts. An author's text is therefore a resemblance to his thoughts, although in terms of biblical text many see the two as identical.

Memory also plays an important role in the representation of thoughts or utterances. The modern academic assumption and expectation of accurate representation would not only have been unknown to the ancients, but is in fact far removed from what is presented and represented in actual life situations, both orally and in print, as even a cursory glance at a newspaper will show.

1. Jack (1999) p. 86.
2. Sacks, J. (2009) *Covenant and Conversation: Genesis*, p. 3.

In spoken or written communication the main principle that creates successful communication is the principle of relevance. The speaker assumes that a hearer listens to what he has to say because she is interested in it: it has relevance for her.[1] That may seem to be overstating the position of the hearer, but in fact we do not merely throw words at one another; those words do relate to situations, contexts in which both speaker and hearer share a common body of knowledge.[2] Humans do not make remarks, or even signs, without an assumption that the hearer will increase her knowledge by listening, or will be able to reassess some information previously held. We listen because we expect relevance, even though we might not articulate it as such. This does not necessarily, or even usually, involve a conscious process, but even a superficial consideration of why we communicate with one another involves the belief that the listener will have some interest in what we have to say. This might not be the perspective of the hearer, or necessarily be of benefit to the hearer, but it will be relevant to her. Even those situations in which a speaker wants to obtain information may give some relevance to a hearer. On many occasions fear makes us unwilling to ask a question, or to ask for help, because of the inferences which the hearer will draw from such a request.[3] The hearer may not want to hear what a speaker has to say but that does not thereby deny its relevance.

Although this may seem to be situationally distinct from the interpretation of biblical text, it does demonstrate the strong role that inference plays in interpreting human behaviour as well as human speech, and, in addition, can be seen to be a factor in certain narrative contexts in these biblical texts.[4] If 'relevance' is the guiding principle in human communication, then we have to take this into account in our understanding of the way in which the authors/text of the Hebrew Bible and the New Testament expected their readers/hearers to make sense of what they were

1. As noted in footnote 2 of p. 2, the speaker or writer will be referred to as 'he', and the hearer or reader as 'she'.
2. If this condition is not fulfilled, then communication *may* fail, but the principle of relevance will lead a hearer to persevere until she 'makes sense' of the utterance.
3. Consider John 4:27; 21:12 and the author's presentation of the disciples as reluctant to ask a question.
4. See Mark 3:1-2; John 4:27; 11:31; Acts 21:27-29 for inferencing which began from viewing actions, or even potential actions.

attempting to communicate. An important part of this approach is the assertion that human communication is *ostensive*; there is an assumption that the communicator intends his utterances to be relevant and understood.

Recent discussion in hermeneutics has focused on whether or not it is possible to have *any* meaning or perhaps any certainty of meaning in a text or utterance. While the debate rages on, the most satisfying account of how humans communicate with one another comes from the field of relevance theory. From this basis we can perhaps draw some hints to progress in the hermeneutical process. Our approach should enable us to examine dialogue and the interaction of the characters presented from a different perspective.

> What relevance theory aims to do is not to produce better interpretations than actual hearers or readers do, but to explain how they arrive at the interpretations they do construct, whether successfully or unsuccessfully.[1]

I will attempt to suggest areas of interpretation for which relevance theory can make a real contribution. I do not attempt to reject earlier scholarship or blaze a trail for a new understanding but rather to give theoretical support for interpretations which might be seen as intuitive rather than evidence based. Relevance theory is concerned with the way in which humans communicate with one another, rather than presenting prescriptive rules for interpretation. The theory claims that hearers make inferences which may not have been intended by the communicator but which seem relevant to them. By examining these I hope to suggest plausible reasons as to why this happens and whether or not this is a feature of canonical texts in particular. The areas I will discuss include the following:

- representation of words or thoughts of others leading on to
- a new perspective on metaphor and
- a new definition of irony;
- particles as guides to interpretation rather than having a fixed lexical meaning;
- logical relations in conditional clauses;
- determining time and aspect.

1. Wilson, D. (2011) 'Relevance and the interpretation of literary works', p. 72 in UCL Working Papers 2011.01 pp. 69-80.

The chapters are arranged to give first of all the theoretical underpinning, followed by particular areas in which relevance theory can be illuminating for biblical studies. Chapter Two then lays out the theoretical basis for the approach to communication known as relevance theory, using biblical texts as examples of these principles. This is set out as a guide for non-linguists with the broad outline of the principles explained and exemplified. This is followed in Chapter Three by an examination of the way in which we re-present the words and thoughts of others, and it considers the question of intertextuality and the role of contextual and encyclopaedic knowledge in communication. Recent scholarly attention to the use of the Old Testament in the New is examined together with the presuppositions that different scholars bring to the topic.

Chapter Four examines the speaker or writer's attitude to re-presentation as seen in echoic utterance or in verbal irony. A new definition of verbal irony is presented and, consequently, an invitation to view certain 'difficult' texts in this light. Some of these include Malachi 1:3, Mark 7:27, and 1 Corinthians 11:19. Furthermore, the misinterpretation that may result if such an attitude is not accurately discerned is clearly laid out. Echoic utterance is examined in the light of recent suggestions for 'difficult' verses in the first Corinthian letter.

Chapter Five examines the way in which particles guide interpretation and relevance, blocking possible wrong inferences and signalling the author's belief concerning, or his desire for, a particular state of affairs. It charts a course in which the instructions a particle gives guide a reader with procedural information, rather than giving a lexical entry for one of these small words. Again, an interpreter's presuppositions may be seen to have greater influence on the text than the function of such particles.

In Chapter Six, the relevance of conditional sentences is examined. The suggestion is that the general or traditional understanding of the syntax of different types of condition as indicating 'true' or 'untrue' situations should be laid aside in exchange for a focus on the principal logical relationship between the two clauses of the conditional sentence. This may make exegesis clearer, and render the preoccupation with 'real' versus 'unreal' and 'true' versus 'untrue' irrelevant, or at least of secondary importance.

A final summary of this new approach and its benefits is laid out in Chapter Seven, together with a brief discussion on the way in which we interpret tense forms and verbal aspect. This has been a hot topic for over twenty-five years and is only touched upon here in conclusion. It is pragmatic inferencing that gives the answer, not a focus on the particular time or aspect.

From Chapter Two onwards, readers should be able not only to view the biblical text with new eyes, but also to reassess their own communication as humans and the way in which this is shaped by 'relevance', even though they may not have considered such a thought before.

I have given my own translations of any Greek, presented so that there should be relevance for all, though the contextual effects for those who can negotiate their way round Koine will be greater.

I have used examples from the *Discourses* of Epictetus to support my argument at several points. Epictetus was the son of a slave woman, and a slave himself, who in later life became a teacher of Stoic philosophy, displaying a severely ascetic life style and a passion for freedom above all else. His dates are uncertain but 50-120CE are the outside limits. His *Discourses* have been recorded by Arrian, who was one of his students, and undertook to note the comments and teaching of his master in the classroom. It does seem as if he made a real attempt to record his teacher's words accurately, our evidence for this view being the Koine grammar in which the teachings are written. Arrian himself wrote in Attic Greek, notwithstanding his centuries of distance from the golden age of Attic writers. I have used Epictetus because there are so many features of his style that resonate with the letters of Paul, particularly his use of diatribe.

Xenophon comes at the end of the classical period, but he also displays features which are found in the New Testament. His work is narrative, and comparable with many other examples in the book.

The translations given from the Greek New Testament text are my own, as are those from Epictetus and Xenophon unless otherwise stated.

Chapter 2
Relevance Theory

This book will make every effort to avoid linguistic terminology, but first we do need to consider the theoretical basis for the claim that the principle of relevance is a valid and useful one for the better understanding of biblical text. Many of the mental exercises biblical scholars engage in when interpreting texts, from mirror reading to a hermeneutic of suspicion, are supported by what I will be outlining here: relevance theory, although biblical scholars may not recognise this. Further, we can employ an 'intuitive' methodology without thought for the premises on which decisions are made. A relevance theory approach gently pushes us to identify such premises or presuppositions and make our argumentation much clearer. Deirdre Wilson points out that

> Much of the interpretation process goes on below the level of consciousness, and although we may find it easy to make intuitive inferences about the communicator's informative and communicative intentions, we cannot discover by introspection how these inferences are made. It is this intuitive ability to infer a communicator's informative and communicative intentions that relevance theorists are trying to describe.[1]

This notion of 'relevance' was first brought to the academic world by the publication of *Relevance* in 1986 by Dan Sperber and Deirdre Wilson, and it marked a very different approach to the interpretation of utterances. A revised edition appeared in 1995 and quotations will be made from this later version.[2] The

1. Wilson (2011) pp. 72-3.
2. Sperber, D. and Wilson, D. (1995) *Relevance: Communication and Cognition*. Oxford: Wiley-Blackwell.

authors claim that the principle which drives communication is that of relevance. They agree that words communicate ideas, but that the principle which decides their interpretation in terms of disambiguating pronomial reference and multiple senses is that of relevance. Put briefly and in colloquial terms, relevance causes us to say as much as we need to and no more. Too much information is a distraction. Relevance is also the principle that guides our interpretation of the speaker's attitude to the information which he is communicating. This last point will be dealt with in a later chapter and has considerable value for the interpretation of biblical material.

If we have not seriously considered the way in which humans communicate, then it might seem as if it is by a so-called 'code model'; namely, that we identify words, put them together and derive the 'meaning'. When we examine this further, however, it really only accounts for a fraction of our communicative effort. Quite apart from body language, we use physical clues such as accent or command of English to aid us in understanding utterances and making assumptions, while even the words we actually utter only form part of the meaning we wish to communicate.

Propositions may be extremely vague, but humans seem to be able to derive meaning from them. The following is a true, though limited, conversation heard on a bus in Glasgow. A woman comes on the bus, sits beside another woman who seems to be known to her, and this exchange takes place:

'This is me since yesterday!'
'Ah'm the same!'

Laconic the first statement might have been but it was obviously relevant to the hearer, who responded accordingly. Others on the bus would draw a range of inferences from this exchange, or, in plain language, they would make an effort to assign a meaning to it. The process we engage in quite unconsciously as we interpret communication seems to be universal and is the basis of the theory we will outline in this book. Although many of the examples of communication practices in Sperber and Wilson's work are oral, the theory they advocate also works well for literature. Deirdre Wilson's paper on 'Relevance and the Interpretation of Literary Works' has already been referred to in Chapter One, but it is worth noting again here that the help RT gives in interpreting literary texts whose authors are long dead is in explaining how such interpretations are arrived at. Wilson acknowledges that 'comprehension necessarily takes place at a risk' but that does not lead to the impossibility of such an attempt to comprehend.

Ian MacKenzie has explored the usefulness of RT in literary criticism in his book *Paradigms of Reading* and also takes account of the special case of canonical texts.

> Relevance Theory is equally able to account for thematic, psychoanalytic, deconstructionist and political interpretations which go way beyond postulated intended meanings.[1]

Canonical works do 'generate alternative interpretations over time', but this does not undermine the expectation of relevance in interpreting texts from an earlier age. MacKenzie quotes Mikhail Bakhtin as recognising that great literary works live on in the future because their roots extend into the distant past.[2] There will be relevance in the interpretations which a later generation propose, but this may not have been the communicative intention of the original author or text. The concept of 'consequences' which arise from the use of ancient texts – particularly sacred or canonical texts – is now being considered much more seriously, but these are not agreed on by all scholars as a necessary corollary of the original text.[3] This book will not attempt to consider these, but the issue is worth noting as tangential to the topic.

RT argues that while a code alone is unable to unlock 'meaning' or relevance, humans infer as an unconscious process whenever they see another human being, and before words have been spoken. This leads on to certain constructs which are involved in our communication, but which we are not normally aware of. These concepts will be unpacked in more detail with examples from biblical texts and other material in Classical and Koine Greek in the following chapters but at this point they

1. MacKenzie, I. (2002) *Paradigms of Reading*. Basingstoke: Palgrave MacMillan, p. 53.
2. Ibid, p. 54.
3. A particularly detailed study of this topic may be found in the commentary on the book of Job by Prof C. Seow, which deals with the derivative art forms arising from some texts in Job which modern readers may consider obscure. Seow, C.L. (2013) *Job 1-21: Interpretation and Commentary*. GR, Michigan: Eerdmans.

will be introduced briefly. Concepts such as **underdeterminacy**, **inferencing**, **metarepresentation** and **ostension** may sound bewildering, but in fact we engage with them in all aspects of our communication in everyday life, as well as in the study of biblical and other literature.

Underdeterminacy

When we say that language is *underdetermined*, we are asserting that humans do not say everything they 'mean' but only what is 'relevant'. A speaker does not have to spell out every single detail of his potential communication. To do so would make communication overloaded and so be less relevant to the hearer, or even as in the example (1c) below to allow her to draw unintended inferences.[1] Consider the following minimal, but extremely common, conversational exchange which is substantially underdetermined in terms of both pronomial reference: who is asking whom, and also missing constituents such as verbs:

(1a) Coffee?
(1b) No, thanks.

Example (1a) requires a substantial amount of inference, but this is supplied by the hearer, presumably from the shared context, who gives in (1b) an equally underdetermined, but communicatively acceptable answer. If a speaker were to say everything he meant, supplying all the referents and completing the grammar, the utterance would become verbose and cause the reader/hearer too much processing effort. Too much processing effort leads to the hearer abandoning the attempt at understanding. Another potential difficulty about making an utterance such as (1b) more explicit, as in (1c) below,

(1c) No, I do not want any coffee, thank you.

is the inference, unintended by the speaker, that a hearer might make, such as: *She is annoyed with me* or *She thinks I'm stupid.*

1. This aspect of RT is developed in much more detail by Robyn Carston (2002) *Thoughts and Utterances.* Oxford: Blackwell p. 28, who points out the extent to which inferencing operates even before an utterance has been completed. She also points out that underdeterminacy may operate at different levels.

Saying more than we require will give rise to unintended inferences such as these, or cause the hearer to abandon the attempt to understand because there is a surfeit of information, much of which could have been inferred. Of course, there are contexts in which a more explicit question would be more appropriate such as 'Would you like to have some coffee?' but the examples in 1a and 1b are very common and very acceptable among friends and colleagues. Sperber and Wilson take this example further by the ambiguous response 'Coffee would keep me awake' to the query 'Coffee?' pointing out that the time at which the answer is given will determine whether or not the responder does or does not need coffee! When a paper has to be completed and the time is near midnight, then coffee might be a very useful thought, but if the responder were anxious to have a good night's sleep then it leads the speaker to infer that the answer will be 'No, thanks'.

In a different context, however, one can envisage a situation in which the single word 'coffee?' with a rising intonation (or a question mark) might indicate a question of identification of something in a jar or packet. These examples are given merely to introduce our ability to infer from an underdetermined communication.

A hearer disambiguates, assigns identity to a referent, or supplies a constituent by making the necessary inferences. Let's take a few examples from biblical text to make this clear.

> Matthew 9:10: And it happened as he was reclining in the house, many tax collectors and 'sinners' came and reclined with Jesus and his disciples.
>
> Mark 2:15: And it happened that while he was reclining in his house, many tax collectors and 'sinners' were reclining with Jesus and his disciples.
>
> Luke 5:29: Levi made a great feast for him in his house.

We regularly identify 'he' and 'his' on the basis of context, but although such referents would have been clearer to the original hearers or readers, a modern reader of Matthew or Mark's account will struggle to assign a referent, particularly in Mark's account where 'he' seems to refer to Jesus but 'his' may be Levi. Some modern translations do identify the character to whom the pronoun refers, but it would be too 'heavy' to have the proper names to which the pronouns refer repeated on every occasion.

Reading only Mark (or Matthew), we might wonder whose house it was, but Luke makes it clear and no doubt the former thought that it *was* clear since there was no other 'relevant' identification; that information about the ownership of the house was irrelevant.

Such underdeterminacy may operate even at word level, with a hearer's background knowledge filling in the more specific information for relevance.[1] We have an interesting example of such underdeterminacy in Acts 19:18:

> πολλοί τε τῶν πεπιστευκότων ἤρχοντο ἐξομολογούμενοι καὶ ἀναγγέλλοντες τὰς πράξεις αὔτων
>
> Many of those who had believed came confessing and announcing their spells/deeds.

The word for 'deeds' may also in certain contexts refer to 'spells' and so in this context in Acts, where spells and magic incantations are in focus, it may be the more relevant translation.[2] This word is, therefore, 'underdetermined', and requires the drawing of inferences from the context to make the communication clearer.

The Greek word χάρις occurs eighteen times in the thirteen chapters of 2 Corinthians, but a glance at a modern translation such as NIV will show that the English renderings of this word include 'grace', benefit', 'thanks', 'service', 'offering', and 'gift'. What is the principle on which these differing renderings are made? One hopes it is relevance, but almost certainly context and perhaps theological assumptions will also play a part. χάρις is substantially underdetermined and a modern reader may lack the context of the culture of benefaction in which the word was used in both Classical and Koine Greek as well as in the wider Greco-Roman world. In RT terms, a reader from that world would have contextual information to guide her but a modern reader requires input to her encyclopaedic knowledge in order to disambiguate this rich word.[3] This word and the concept which it evokes is the subject of a substantial volume by John Barclay, in which the original background is taken seriously in the Greek,

---

1. The way in which a hearer or reader assigns a particular value to a word will be discussed in more detail later in this chapter.
2. This is suggested by C.K. Barrett (1994) *A Critical and Exegetical Commentary on the Acts of the Apostles* vol. 2. Edinburgh: T. & T. Clarke. ICC. p. 912.
3. Barclay, J.M.G (2015) *Paul and the Gift*. GR, Michigan: Eerdmans.

Roman and Jewish world. Barclay suggests the 'perfections' of grace which different cultures and various theologies assume to be normative. These differ widely, and there is no space to discuss these in this small book, but Barclay's work is important not least because he deals with assumptions held but never examined, as well as opening up the fascinating world of social relationships in the ancient world.

This underdeterminacy works for grammatical forms also. In both Classical and Koine Greek, participles are underdetermined in terms of their logical relationship to the rest of the sentence, but the context guides a reader to a relevant reading.[1] Translations will add 'when', 'because', 'although', 'as if', to such participles in order to explicate these relationships. Occasionally there may be more than one reading with a reader's own presuppositions contributing to the disambiguation. Greek also has certain small particles which guide or constrain interpretation and these will be discussed in Chapter Five.

This feature of communication leads on to the next necessary step which humans make unconsciously, but all the time: inferencing. The anthropologist Daniel Sperber comments:

> Do humans infer? Do birds fly?[2]

In human society we make inferences before any words are spoken, and in fact almost as soon as we see another human being. At this point, we should consider the inferencing necessary to make verbal communication possible.

Inferences

If language is underdetermined, then a hearer or reader has to supply information from her encyclopaedic knowledge or from the general context. The speaker or writer provides a stimulus in the form of certain words, but then the contextual information enables the hearer to build up her understanding of the speaker's communicative intention. The physical environment or earlier

1. This is dealt with in M.G. Sim (2004) 'Underdeterminacy in Greek participles' in *Bible Translator* 55 pp. 348-359, as well as in Chapter Five.
2. Sperber, D. (1994) 'Understanding Verbal Understanding', p. 188 in J. Khalfa (ed.) *What is Intelligence?* Cambridge: CUP, pp. 179-98.

communication between the communicators may account for such contextual information, as in the earlier examples about coffee. Further, there will be a body of information which is shared by a wider community: shared contextual assumptions. Both contextual information and shared contextual assumptions aid the speaker in communicating and the hearer in interpreting utterances. As twenty-first century readers we need to consider what the original hearers would have inferred from the following description in Acts 16:13:

> On the Sabbath we went out of the gate to the river where we thought there was prayer, and sitting down we spoke with the women who had gathered there.

Firstly, the pronoun 'we': is it 'Luke' the author as well as Paul who is the central character in this narrative? Pronomial reference helps to make a narrative cohesive but we do need to assign identity to such pronouns. Then there are implicatures which might include the following:[1]

- Jews meet together to pray on the Sabbath
- ten men are needed to form a synagogue
- if there was no synagogue, Jews or God fearers might meet outside the town
- those meeting might choose a site near water for reasons of purification, and so on.

All this information would be brought to the text from the encyclopaedic knowledge and contextual assumptions of the original hearers. A relevant meaning is still possible without such knowledge, but the contextual effects are richer when these implicatures are worked out. Even the reference to a 'gate' is opaque to modern readers. This knowledge is part of the 'meaning', but it is brought to the text by the reader or hearer and not by a code discernible from the words in the narrative. Hearers *do* try to make sense of what they hear: this is an intrinsic part of human communication. We do not merely throw words at one another. RT describes this process as *mutual parallel adjustment* in which a reader will enrich a

1. Clark (2013) 'implicatures are communicated assumptions which are not explicitly communicated', p. 217.

proposition by supplying referents and adjusting temporal and ambiguous content as well as 'working out implicit content'.[1] She will continue to derive inferences in her attempt to find relevance until the processing effort seems to be greater than the information to be communicated. At this point the hearer stops processing, and abandons the attempt to understand since the principle of relevance has not been met.

Of course, a hearer may be unaware of the original context and assume that her own context is similar. Some Ethiopian readers, when discussing the accusation John the Baptist made against Herod for 'taking his brother's wife', assume that John was opposed to wife inheritance.[2] The fact that Herod's brother was still alive would not have been part of their encyclopaedic knowledge, but the fact of wife inheritance is part of their contextual information. It seems incredible to them that someone could 'take' his brother's wife while that brother was still alive. Nevertheless, that is what had happened, and was the reason for John the Baptist's accusation.

If there are several possible interpretations of an utterance, a hearer will derive the most easily accessible, which RT defines as the most relevant. I overheard the following dialogue some years ago, and it is used with permission:

> 'I studied Greek for 4 years in Athens.'
> 'Wow!'

The hearer has inferred from the words 'Greek' and 'Athens' that the speaker studied in the capital city of Greece. For her, that is the most easily accessible interpretation, given the use of the words 'Greek' and 'Athens'. In spite of this reasonable assumption, the actual place in which the speaker studied was Athens, Georgia, USA. This is *not* an inference which a non-American would find readily accessible, and even for an American, the most *relevant* interpretation would still locate the place of study as Greece. Furthermore, the physical context of a biblical research centre in which the conversation took place led the hearer to assume that the speaker had studied Koine Greek, whereas in a different context the natural assumption would be that the

1. Clark (2013) p. 121. Clark has many helpful examples of the benefit of deriving explicatures on pages 224-7.
2. Matthew 14:3-4.

language in question was Modern Greek. On the other hand, the speaker knew that the hearer would react in this way and made no attempt to clarify the location until the conversation continued.

In literature, authors frequently lead a reader in a certain direction by a conversation or setting. As the narrative progresses, the reader has to retrace her steps because conflicting information is then presented. Seiji Uchida comments:

> In detective novels or mysteries it is often the case that strong implicatures are intentionally communicated to the reader. At the same time, other assumptions are weakly implicated so that finally the reader's expectations are betrayed.[1]

Uchida goes on to suggest that such strategies, or 'twists', as she terms them, create 'poetic effects'. This will be discussed in more detail in Chapter Three, but many authors do lead a reader to infer certain facts. At a later stage these facts have to be adjusted, and this is not only the case with detective or mystery novels, but with a wider range of literature, too.[2]

Historically, biblical studies has put emphasis on understanding the original context of the text as an essential prerequisite for interpretation, while more recent approaches have allowed readings which would not have been immediately recognisable to an 'original' audience. RT looks at the text as it stands, with no attempt to go behind it in order to discern the identity of the author, authorial intent, or date of composition, apart from the assumption that the presence of a text assumes an intention to communicate on the part of 'someone'.

Of course, there are issues of provenance and language to be considered, but my purpose in writing this book is to demonstrate a fresh way of considering text using modern methods of communication and cognition. I want to look at the text from the perspective of such methods and to view it as a whole in its final form without attempting to dissect the layers of composition.

As we will see below, the reader may employ the strategy of 'sophisticated understanding' in order to read another agenda

1. Uchida, S. (1998) 'Text and Relevance' in S. Uchida & R. Carston (eds.) *Relevance Theory: Applications and Implications*. Amsterdam: John Benjamins, pp. 161-178.
2. Uchida cites Ernest Hemingway and John Grisham in this connection, but the practice is widespread.

behind the 'intention' of the author. Nevertheless, the theory requires shared contextual information for communication to be successful. By 'successful', I am stating that the hearer or reader will obtain new information or have information previously held strengthened. There is no possibility that I can claim that 'successful' implies that the speaker or writer has communicated to his hearer the exact thoughts which were in his mind as he spoke, wrote or dictated. This takes us back to the questions of background: geographical, historical, social, and cultural, not to mention the theological presuppositions that earlier readers might have been expected to share with the author. These are all part of what RT calls *encyclopaedic information.* The inferences a reader draws from a text are contingent on the factors mentioned. The readers who do not share or have access to this information will draw different inferences from that text. It may still be relevant but in a different way.

This is usefully illustrated by the way in which the Church Fathers interpreted the parables. For them allegory was a natural, even an essential, communicative strategy and the identification of every detail of the story was necessary in order to obtain maximum relevance. Western scholars are extremely wary of such a strategy, but readers from other parts of the world find it useful because it draws out potential meaning from the illustration, giving a fresh outlook on an ancient text. We may feel that this exercise is an illegitimate application of a text, but that distinction is not recognised everywhere.

Metarepresentation

In communication, writers and speakers frequently make use of utterances made by someone else. Of course, if this is being reported as such, the conventions of quotation marks – even 'finger dancing' in oral communication – will be a useful aid for the reader. In many cases, however, a speaker will re-present what he or someone else has said or thought not in exact words but in a 'loose resemblance'. This will be dealt with in Chapter Three, but is introduced here as being a vital part of the communicative process which we all use but are seldom aware of. It is also an important part of interpreting biblical text, but is in general unidentified as re-presentation.

Our utterances resemble our thoughts, but they are not the *same* as our thoughts. This will also be expanded later but is raised here because when we re-present, as stated above, we frequently give a loose resemblance which fits our understanding of the relevance of the communication.

If utterances are a representation of human thought, then humans must be communicating such representations both of their own thought, and that of others. Humour and advertising rely heavily on this ability to re-present and these will fail if the audience does not recognise this, for example, in cross-cultural or different physical situations. Additionally, if the representation is not recognised but taken as the words of the speaker, then the potential for serious misunderstanding arises.

A recent example from the *Daily Telegraph* shows this very clearly. The UK Business Secretary in 2013, Vince Cable, was quoted as follows:

> News of the planned meeting emerged after Mr Cable's surprise attack on the Bank for acting like the 'capital Taliban' by demanding lenders armour plate their balance sheet against losses.[1]

The quotation marks in the article imply that Mr Cable had used this phrase, but an earlier article in the Financial Times shows that what Vince Cable actually said was

> . . . the so-called 'capital Taliban' in the Bank of England are imposing restrictions.

In other words, Mr Cable was in fact quoting someone else who had called the Bank of England the 'capital Taliban'. The use of 'so-called' distances the speaker from the term, but when it is removed it gives an erroneous impression of Mr Cable's comments and makes them more forceful, particularly when used with words such as 'attack'. The use of such a metaphor as 'Taliban' is powerful, bringing contextual implications of legalism and forceful implementation. Metaphor and the concept of close and loose resemblance will be dealt with in the next chapter.

Other phrases such as 'seemingly' and 'apparently' fulfil similar functions in distancing a speaker from a proposition,

1. *Daily Telegraph* of 24th July 2013.

and these are called ‘evidentials’ in RT.[1] The speaker makes no claim concerning the truth or accuracy of the statement, but is reporting what he has heard.

In the New Testament the word δοκέω similarly distances the speaker from the truth or otherwise of the comment. It is a signal to receive the presentation with caution. Its use in Galatians 2:6 leads the reader to infer the reservations that Paul has about the standing of ‘those who seemed to be something’. The passive form of λέγω is used frequently to indicate how someone is named, or how a name or phrase is translated, but may also in certain context indicate the distancing of the speaker from such an attribution. This is probably, or most relevantly, its use in 1 Corinthians 8:5:

> καὶ γὰρ εἴπερ εἰσὶν λεγόμενοι θεοὶ εἴτε ἐν οὐρανῷ εἴτε ἐπὶ γῆς, ὥσπερ εἰσιν θεοὶ πολλοὶ καὶ κύριοι πολλοί, ἀλλ’ ἡμῖν εἷς θεὸς . . .
>
> For even if there are so-called gods whether in heaven or on earth as there are many gods and lords, but for us there is one God . . .

From Epictetus’ *Discourses*:

> οἱ βασιλεῖς λεγόμενοι
>
> those called ‘kings’ (MGS)
> those who are styled kings (Oldfather)[2]

The use of a passive form by removing the agent will also distance the writer or speaker from agreement with such a description:

> Οἱ βασιλεῖς τῶν ἐθνῶν κυριεύουσιν αὐτῶν καὶ οἱ ἐξουοσιάζοντες αὐτῶν εὐεργέται καλοῦνται.
>
> The kings of the nations lord it over them and those who have authority over them are called ‘benefactors’.[3]

By using a passive form here, the speaker is making no statement about whether or not he agrees with such an appellation. Of course,

1. Ifantidou, E. (2001) has discussed this in detail in *Evidentials and Relevance*. Amsterdam: John Benjamins.
2. 4.1.51.
3. Luke 22:25.

it may also be taken as Middle Voice – 'they call themselves' – but that is even more transparently the ascription of 'those who have authority', rather than the speaker.

A speaker, unless he is talking to himself, makes his intention to communicate clear by both physical signs and vocal indicators. Even when we see someone using sign language parallel to a public speaker, we infer that this person is communicating the same information as the speaker to an audience who are unable to hear. This intention is called 'ostension' in RT, and we will unpack its input now.

Ostension

Ostension is behaviour on the part of the communicator that indicates that he intends to make something manifest to the hearer. In simple terms, a speaker by his behaviour lets someone hearing him know that he intends to communicate with her. In written texts, if an author takes time and effort to produce a record of his thoughts, beliefs or experiences, I suggest that this indicates his intention to make these known or 'manifest' to other parties, those who will read such a record. This may be in doubt in the case of private journals, but even with these, the author may have a vague idea of passing these on to others as a record of personal experiences, or at least of having the opportunity himself to revisit past thoughts.

In the example above which deals with the underdeterminacy of 'Greek' and 'Athens', the speaker knows that the hearer has recovered the most *relevant* interpretation for her; indeed, he has guided her to it by the use of 'Greek' and 'Athens'. The hearer may not even have been aware that there was another Athens in Georgia, USA. This is called *ostensive* behaviour: the speaker intended the hearer to draw this conclusion. In this example, the hearer was then willing to explain the context when it was misunderstood, but, as we shall see below, there are occasions when a speaker may deliberately lead a hearer to infer one interpretation that he, the speaker, knows to be untrue.

This expectation of communication is so much part of what we take for granted in conversation and social interaction that its significance may be ignored. When we understand what is involved, we can see that while a speaker may intend to communicate one proposition, the hearer may suspect that he has an ulterior motive in his communicative strategy. The example below from John 12:5-6 is a good model for what is being communicated ostensively, where the hearers are suspicious rather than being impressed.

> Δὶα τί τοῦτο τὸ μύρον οὐκ ἐπράθη τριακοσίων δηναρίων καὶ ἐδόθη πτωχοῖς;
> εἶπεν δὲ τοῦτο οὐχ ὅτι περὶ τῶν πτωχῶν ἔμελεν αὐτῷ, ἀλλ' ὅτι κλέπτης ἦν καὶ τὸ γλωσσόκομον ἔχων τὰ βαλλόμενα ἐβάσταζεν.
>
> 'Why was this perfume not sold for 300 denarii and (the proceeds) given to the poor?'
> He said this not because he cared about the poor but because he was a thief and (holding the bag) being the treasurer kept what was put in.

Strategies for Interpretation

We have claimed that humans do try to make sense of utterances and there are three basic strategies for doing so. The first is described as *naïve optimism* – this is the 'path of least effort'. The interpretation that is the most relevant to the hearer is the one selected. It could be thought that the interpretation of the disciples of an enigmatic saying of Jesus in Matthew 16:5-7 was driven by naïve optimism, or rather the most relevant interpretation for them:

> When the disciples went to the other side (of the lake) they forgot to take bread. Jesus said to them, 'Take care and beware of the yeast of the Pharisees and Sadducees'. But the disciples were discussing and saying among themselves, 'We did not take bread'.

The disciples were disabused of this interpretation but the text presents it as the easiest to access for them because of the link between 'yeast' and 'bread'.

If naïve optimism does not produce a 'relevant' understanding, then a hearer will move on to *cautious optimism*. In this approach, the hearer believes that the speaker is being truthful, but is perhaps not as competent as he should be in his communicative strategy. The hearer, therefore, will move on to the next most relevant interpretation. In normal human communication this is very common, as may be seen by the way in which we finish the sentences of a speaker who hesitates, or correct a word which is 'wrong' to our understanding.

One example from John 7:34 shows the struggle for comprehension on the part of those who heard Jesus talk about going away where they are unable to follow him:

> 'You will look for me, but you will not find me; and where I am you cannot come.'
>
> The Jews said to one another, 'Where does this man intend to go that we cannot find him? Will he go where our people live scattered among the Greeks, and teach the Greeks? What did he mean when he said "You will look for me, but you will not find me" and "Where I am you cannot come"?'

Humans assume that what is being addressed to them makes sense and they will either struggle until they find a relevant interpretation, or give up the attempt if the effort is greater than the potential interpretation.

Should the hearer suspect, however, that the speaker is *not* being truthful ('benevolent' in the terminology of Sperber), she will move on to a *sophisticated understanding* of the communication.[1] Some hearers are much more inclined to take this path which treats with suspicion the intentions of the speaker. The hearer knows that the speaker wants her to process the information with naïve optimism, but suspects strongly that he has another agenda. A sophisticated understanding should be able to uncover the speaker's real communicative intention (*he wants me to believe that . . .*), perhaps by using other relevant contextual or encyclopaedic information. A good example of this which I quoted earlier may be seen in John 12:5-6:

> Δὶα τί τοῦτο τὸ μύρον οὐκ ἐπράθη τριακοσίων δηναρίων καὶ ἐδόθη πτωχοῖς;
>
> εἶπεν δὲ τοῦτο οὐχ ὅτι περὶ τῶν πτωχῶν ἔμελεν αὐτῷ, ἀλλ' ὅτι κλέπτης ἦν καὶ τὸ γλωσσόκομον ἔχων τὰ βαλλόμενα ἐβάσταζεν.

1. Sperber (1994) pp. 179-198.

> 'Why was this perfume not sold for 300 denarii and (the proceeds) given to the poor?'
>
> He said this not because he cared about the poor but because he was a thief and (holding the bag) being the treasurer kept what was put in.

The author is refusing the motivation of care for the poor which was presented by Judas as a reason for selling the ointment rather than pouring it out on Jesus. In many ways, such a strategy resembles the biblical studies' concept of a 'hermeneutic of suspicion', in which a hearer knows that she is expected to believe what was presented to her, but she discerns another agenda. One other well known example of this is seen in Matthew 2:8:

> Sending them (the Magi) to Bethlehem Herod said, 'Go and make a careful search for the child. As soon as you find him, report to me, so that I too may go and worship him.'

The Magi took his words at face value (naïve optimism) but the narrative shows that they were warned in a dream about the intentions of Herod. Readers guided by the earlier narrative of Herod 'being disturbed' will employ a different strategy, being suspicious of Herod's ostensive desire to worship someone other than himself and, in the case of the first readers, by their encyclopaedic knowledge of that absolute monarch.

Clark has a useful summary of the expectation of relevance with each of these strategies:

> an interpreter who is a naive optimist will expect actual relevance, a cautious optimist will expect attempted relevance and a sophisticated understander will expect purported relevance.[1]

Relevance Theory Simplified

Relevance theory is theoretically much more complex than the initial presentation I have given here. I have deliberately avoided discussions of explicatures and implicatures at this point, feeling that if we grasp the concept of language being underdetermined, and this underdeterminacy being resolved by the inferences which a hearer will make when presented with a less than

1. Clark (2013) p. 351.

complete utterance, we will be able to make use of the theory to great benefit. Of course, such discussions are the life blood of linguists, but for non-linguists they can seem intimidating. The truly wonderful thing about RT is that it works! It is actually true to human behaviour and expectations, in describing how we not only make sense of words and phrases, but also body language. Furthermore, it gives a very good account of the way in which communication may fail and this is true not only to personal experience, but to the many examples in the biblical text which substantiate the value of such an account. I give a few of these 'misunderstandings' below.

Misunderstanding in Verbal and Non-Verbal Communication

We have said that humans infer as soon as they see another human being, before a single word is spoken. Gestures and body language work only by inference. Cross-culturally, these can be misinterpreted: gestures such as winking or giggling are interpreted very differently across cultures, but within a culture, the one gesturing usually assumes that the observer finds his actions relevant because of their shared cultural assumptions. What makes such communication successful when no words are spoken? The answer is relevance. This can be seen in several narrative situations, in particular in the account narrated in John 11:28-31. Here Mary has been informed by Martha that Jesus has arrived in the village, and so she gets up to go to him. Those watching her made the following assumption:

> So when the Jews who were with her in the house, grieving with her saw Mary get up quickly and go out, they followed her thinking that she was going to her brother's grave to weep there.[1]

This was a very reasonable inference drawn from the behaviour of this grieving woman, but it was wrong because those who drew it had not heard the whispered conversation of Martha with her sister.

Acts 21:28-29 has a much more serious misunderstanding in which bystanders are said to have assumed that when Paul went into the temple he had taken in with him a non-Jew, on the grounds that they had seen him previously in the city with an Ephesian man. This wrong assumption led to a serious riot.

1. John 11:31, my translation.

Do humans infer? All the time, and they do not always draw the correct inferences.

In other passages the picking up of stones signifies a desire to do harm, or at the very least it is intimidating, as in John 8:59:

> So they lifted stones to throw at him, but Jesus hid and went away from the temple.

And again in John 10:31:

> The Jews/Judeans again picked up stones to stone him. Jesus responded to them, I have shown you many good works from the Father. For which of these are you stoning me?

In both of these examples the act of picking up stones was interpreted as a preliminary to attack, and even, in the second example, as judicial killing for blasphemy, since the verb λιθάζω is used three times in this and the following verses.[1] The act of picking up stones was ostensive. It would have been seen as such in a first-century context, indicating, as made clear in the subsequent response of the potential attackers, a judgement on perceived blasphemy.

A more complicated example in Acts 14:8-18 describes the reactions of onlookers to a healing miracle when they did not understand the language being spoken by those engaged in the healing. The encyclopaedic and contextual background of those living in Lystra caused them to infer a status for Paul and Barnabas which was completely mistaken, but in their context it was the most relevant understanding of what they had witnessed without understanding the verbal communication which accompanied the actions: 'when they saw what Paul had done'.[2]

We noted that underdeterminacy may operate down to the level of individual words and the ambiguity of the word κοιμάομαι in Greek meaning either literal or metaphorical 'sleep', the latter being a euphemism for death, creates another example of communication which seemed to fail initially.

---

1. In pagan Greek this verb describes merely throwing stones, but in the NT context, with the background of the Hebrew Bible, it includes the concept of punishment for certain offences including blasphemy and adultery.
2. Acts 14:11. The story told by Ovid of an elderly couple who entertained Jupiter and Mercury unawares may be the background to this misunderstanding.

> λέγει αὐτοῖς, Λάζαρος ὁ φίλος ἡμῶν κεκοίμηται· ἀλλὰ πορεύομαι ἵνα ἐξυπνίσω. εἶπαν οὖν οἱ μαθηταὶ αὐτῷ, Κύριε, εἰ κεκοίμηται σωθήσεται. εἰρήκει δὲ ὁ Ἰησοῦς περὶ τοῦ θανάτου αὐτοῦ, ἐκεῖνοι δὲ ἔδοξαν ὅτι περὶ τῆς κοιμήσεως τοῦ ὕπνου λέγει.
>
> He said to them, 'Lazarus our friend has fallen asleep, but I am going to waken him.' So the disciples said to him, 'Lord, if he has fallen asleep he will be healed.' Jesus by contrast had been speaking about his death but they thought that he was speaking about the rest of sleep (the sleeping of sleep).

Summary

This chapter has briefly outlined the theoretical underpinning of relevance theory, not in the same detail a linguist requires, but with sufficient examples of the basic constructs involved to enable a biblical scholar to use it beneficially in the interpretation of text. Let me summarise what Deirdre Wilson outlines concerning what RT does and does not claim to do in examining literary texts:

> What relevance theory aims to do is not to produce better interpretations than actual hearers or readers do, but to explain how they arrive at the interpretations they do construct, whether successfully or unsuccessfully.[1]

We will now move on to particular topics that relevance theory can inform and illuminate.

1. Wilson (2011) pp. 69-80.

Chapter 3
Re-presentation

In the two previous chapters, we have discussed the way in which we make sense of words and utterances, not merely by deciphering each word, but by adding inferences drawn from contextual information and encyclopaedic knowledge. A further dimension of the communication strategy of a speaker or writer is the work of putting thoughts into words. This is a vital but generally ignored aspect of communication.

In describing the way in which speakers communicate with one another, RT claims that every utterance, spoken or written, is a *re-presentation* of the thought of the speaker or writer. In stating this, the theory does not examine the detail of the way in which the mind converts thought into utterance, but limits itself to dealing with the result of such re-presentation. This may seem a quite unnecessary step to most of us, since we may assume that we encapsulate our thoughts into words which give an exact representation of our thoughts, but this is not the case.

Writers on RT go into much more detail concerning this process, and the way in which thoughts are converted to concepts and concepts to linguistic forms which are then subject to inferencing. For the purpose of this discussion, let's begin with the assertion that utterances *resemble our thoughts* as they re-present them, but they do not represent them in an exact form, only a resemblance to that thought.

As explained in the previous chapter, the one who hears such an utterance will make inferences from the linguistic forms used in order to understand what the speaker intends to communicate. As we communicate, however, we regularly re-present not only our own thoughts, but the thoughts of others, either by direct or indirect speech, thus claiming to *re-present* the utterance of the speaker or writer. In addition to this conscious representation, however, we frequently do this with *no conscious thought of the fact of re-presentation.* I want to examine direct, indirect and 'unconscious' representation separately in this chapter, because all three forms are regularly bundled together by biblical scholars in discussing how New Testament writers – in particular Paul – 'use the Old Testament'. Allusion, echo, and intentionality are part of the ongoing debate on this topic, and these will be dealt with later in this chapter.

Direct Speech

Sperber and Wilson point out that 'direct quotations are the most obvious examples of utterances used to represent not what they describe but what they resemble.'[1] This needs to be constantly borne in mind, since the expectation of exact resemblance is a modern notion.[2] Even when direct speech is marked as such by textual punctuation, expectations of faithful representation are a modern phenomenon. The lengthy speeches found in the works of Thucydides, Xenophon and others are most unlikely to have been represented in the exact form in which they were spoken, although Polybius, criticising other historians, claims that *he* was reporting what was actually said.[3] The comments of Thucydides on his methodology in dealing with lengthy speeches are well known:

> With reference to the speeches in this history, some were delivered before the war began, others while it was going on; some I heard myself, others I got from various quarters; it was in all cases difficult to carry them word for word in one's memory, so my habit has been to make the speaker say what was in my opinion demanded of them by the various occasions, of course adhering as closely as possible to the general sense of what they really said.[4]

1. Sperber and Wilson (1995) p. 228.
2. Direct quotation has been referred to more recently as *metalinguistic representation*, because of the close resemblance between the original and the quotation. Gutt (2004) unpublished paper, Almazan Garcia (2002).
3. οἱ κατ' ἀλήθειαν εἰρημένοι λόγοι – *The Histories* 12.25b.1.
4. Thucydides, *History of the Peloponnesian War*, 1.22.1 LCL 108. Trans. R. Crawley, 1910. London: J.M. Dent.

Regarding the modern assumption of exact correspondence, I am making this point to clear the ground for a recognition that 'close resemblance' – to use the RT term – is the most that we should expect and this is not an unreasonable expectation.

As well as direct quotations, however, we refer to the beliefs or comments of others regularly, not only by prefacing the utterance with an introductory 'She said . . .' but also by referring to what we have been told tangentially in the form of evidentials.[1] As noted in Chapter Two, in the second chapter of Galatians Paul uses δοκέω three times, and in so doing distances himself from an opinion about those who were leaders or 'thought to be something'.[2] He re-presents this belief, but by using this Greek verb he distances himself from that opinion. Paul also represents Apollos as being unwilling to visit the Corinthians at this time, but 'he will come whenever it is suitable'.[3] We do not know what Apollos actually said, but Paul is interpreting his thoughts or his comments in this way.

There are several interesting examples of this in non-biblical literature. Take the following example in *Mansfield Park*, one of many from Jane Austen:

> Though the weather was hot, there were shady lanes wherever they wanted to go. A young party is always provided with a shady lane.[4]

The context shows that several of the characters were determined to go on an expedition which the wiser among them felt was injudicious given the very hot weather. This excerpt is echoic in RT terms, but verges on irony (see Chapter Four) where the author states what at first seems to be her own opinion but which is in fact that of some of her characters.

Such representation, which in essence claims to be the words of another, is said to be *interpretively used*. In addition to reporting the utterances of others, humans also seem to attribute to them

1. These may be asides such as 'it seems', 'evidently', 'apparently' etc. but they all presuppose an utterance by a third party. The speaker is not taking responsibility for his own comments, but attributing them to another. Elly Ifantidou (2001) deals with this.
2. Galatians 2:2, 6, 9.
3. 1 Corinthians 16:12.
4. Austen, J. (1833) *Mansfield Park*, London: Richard Bentley. p. 62.

thoughts and intentions, thus *interpretively representing* their thought: 'Humans can no more refrain from attributing intentions than they can from batting their eyelids.'[1]

Consider the following descriptions and then attributions of 'purpose':

a) George said, 'I live in Luxembourg to avoid paying taxes in the UK.'
b) George said that he lived in Luxembourg to avoid paying taxes in the UK.
c) George lives in Luxembourg to avoid paying taxes in the UK.

Example (a) and (b) represent in direct (a) and indirect speech (b) a purpose that George stated. In example (b), there is an element of interpretation, in that the quotation is not verbatim, but interprets George's utterance. In both (a) and (b), George may not have been telling the truth, or he may have been using irony: for example, he may be quoting a colleague's understanding of his living arrangements.[2] The speaker, however, makes no claim about the truth value of George's statement. He merely reports it descriptively (a) or interpretively (b). In example (c), however, the speaker attributes a purpose to George which does not claim to be based on his utterance, although it may be, but on the speaker's inference from George's action. The speaker's utterance is therefore a re-presentation of a thought he had about the intention of George:[3]

Speaker's thought: *George lives in Luxembourg to avoid paying taxes in the UK.*
George's thought as inferred by the speaker: *If I live in Luxembourg I will avoid paying taxes in the UK.*

---

1. Sperber (1994) p. 187.
2. See Noh, E.J (2000) *Metarepresentation.* Amsterdam: John Benjamins, for further discussion of the RT approach to irony dealt with here in Chapter Four.
3. The term 'metarepresentation' is used throughout RT literature, but for ease of communication I have simplified this to 'representation'. The reader should understand that this description may indicate several orders of representation: that is, it may indicate a representation of a representation. Although this simplification may not be acceptable to linguists, it has seemed to me to be necessary in presenting this concept to a wider audience.

In addition, then, to re-presenting our own thoughts and the utterances of others descriptively, we may also represent the thoughts of others *interpretively*, attributing intention to them which they may or may not acknowledge, as in (c). This is very clear again in Galatians 6:13:

> θέλουσιν ὑμᾶς περιτέμνεσθαι, ἵνα ἐν τῇ ὑμετέρᾳ σαρκὶ καυχήσθνται.
>
> They want you to be circumcised so that they may boast in your flesh.

The clause introduced by the particle ἵνα represents an intention or potential state of affairs on the part of the subject of the sentence: 'we may boast in your flesh'. Now, almost certainly the subjects would not have agreed that this was their purpose or intention, but Paul ascribes it to them as he does also in 4:17 of the same letter. As noted above, this seems to be what humans do on a regular basis, with or without evidence.

Sperber[1] claims that all speakers have such interpretive abilities, although it is also acknowledged that people displaying certain syndromes such as Asperger's or autism may not have developed the ability to access more complex re-presentation.[2] It has also been observed that very young children do not re-present beyond such level: ironic utterances are usually wasted on young children, as most parents will realise. Nevertheless, the understanding of the crucial role which re-presentation plays in the interpretation of utterances, and of course in communication in general, is a major component in biblical interpretation.

Further, we may make an utterance about the real world, that is, about a *state of affairs* in the real world, or, alternatively, we may express our attitude to the real world or to a potential situation, described as a *potential state of affairs.* Consider the following example:

1. Sperber (1994) p. 187.
2. This aspect of RT is dealt with in much more detail in Wilson (2000) 'Metarepresentation in linguistic communication' in D. Sperber (ed.) *Metarepresentations: An Interdisciplinary Perspective.* Oxford: OUP, pp. 411-48, which includes extracts from L.H. Willey (1999) *Pretending to be Normal: Living with Asperger's Syndrome.* London: Jessica Kingsley Publishers.

Peter came to the house today.

This utterance *represents* the speaker's thought, but is a description of an observable situation in the real world: a state of affairs. If, on the other hand, a speaker says,

I wanted Peter to come to the house today.

he may be 'describing' in saying 'I wanted', but in the following clause he is not describing an actual 'state of affairs' but *representing* a *desirable* state of affairs.[1] This desirable state of affairs might never happen. The utterance indicates the speaker's attitude to a potential state of affairs: Peter coming to the house.

At the heart of re-presentation, whether of our own thoughts or re-presenting the thoughts of others, is the concept of the transfer of thought to utterance. As noted in Chapter Two, we may assume that we say what we are thinking, that our thoughts and utterances are identical, but in fact that cannot be proved. An utterance as a representation of a thought will then be enriched by the recovery of inferences which should lead the hearer or reader to an understanding of the communicative intention of the speaker/writer. Sometimes, in order to make a re-presentation more salient, procedural markers will be used to highlight the interpretive nature of the utterance. These will be considered in more detail in Chapter Five.

When a speaker re-presents someone else's utterance and expresses his attitude towards it, that re-presentation is said to be *echoic* in RT terms. Consider a very simple example of this:

A: 'I'm going to town tomorrow.'
B: 'You're going to town tomorrow?'

Here B is not merely repeating what A has just said, but in repeating is giving rise to her attitude and several weak inferences, such as: B is astonished at this information or B is relating this utterance to her own agenda, and plans that A do something for her while in town.

Frequently, a hearer may echo a previous utterance in order to disagree with it, or express surprise at its content. Consider

1. It will be seen that in Koine Greek writers frequently chose to mark such representation of a 'desirable' state of affairs by the use of ἵνα with the subjunctive. This will be dealt with in Chapter Five.

the following dialogue in John 8:56, from many similar in the same chapter:

> Ἀβραὰμ ὁ πατὴρ ὑμῶν ἠγαλλιάσατο ἵνα ἴδῃ τὴν ἡμέραν τὴν ἐμήν, καὶ εἶδεν καὶ ἐχάρη.
> εἶπον οὖν οἱ Ἰουδαῖοι πρὸς αὐτὸν, Πεντήκοντα ἔτη οὔπω ἔχεις καὶ Ἀβραὰμ ἑώρακας;
>
> 'Abraham your father was glad that he should see my day; he both saw it and rejoiced.' So the Judeans said to him, 'You are not yet fifty and you have seen Abraham?'

The repetition here is not verbatim, but is a loose resemblance of the first utterance. The attitude of the respondents to the first utterance is clear: they echo in order to express incredulity. Of course, the subject is reversed: 'You have seen Abraham?' rather than 'Abraham saw my day', but it may be seen as a reasonably logical assumption that if Abraham had seen Jesus then Jesus must have seen Abraham![1]

Indirect Speech

Since Koine Greek introduces both direct and indirect speech by the particle ὅτι, it is only pragmatic clues such as pronomial reference which help us to distinguish the two forms. The particle is nevertheless an indication to the reader of a representation and in certain texts the two forms are combined as we can see from the following examples:

> ἔρχεται Μαριὰμ ἡ Μαγδαληνὴ ἀγγέλλουσα τοῖς μαθηταῖς ὅτι ἑώρακα τὸν κύριον, καὶ ταῦτα εἶπεν αὐτῇ.
>
> Mary Magdalene comes announcing to the disciples 'I have seen the Lord' and he spoke these words (things) to her.
>
> καὶ συναλιζόμενος παρήγγειλεν αὐτοῖς ἀπὸ Ἱεροσολύμων μὴ χωρίζεσθαι ἀλλὰ περιμένειν τὴν ἐπαγγελίαν τοῦ πατρὸς ἥν ἠκουσατέ μου, ὅτι ὁ Ἰωάννης μὲν ἐβάπτισεν ὕδατι, ὑμεῖς δὲ ἐν πνεύματι βαπτισθήσεσθε ἁγίῳ οὐ μετὰ πολλὰς ταύτας ἡμέρας.

---

1. It is worth noting that there is a variant reading ἑώρακεν σε; 'he saw you?' for this echo.

> Gathering them together he instructed them not to leave Jerusalem but to wait for 'the promise from the Father which you heard from me that John baptised in water but you will be baptised with the Holy Spirit not many days ahead.'[1]

This particle ὅτι will be considered in Chapter Five, but although it signals a representation we discern whether that is direct or indirect by the pragmatics of the sentence as noted above. It has been commonly understood in the past by naïve readers that the indication in a text of direct speech, as compared with indirect, claims to be an accurate transcription of dialogue or teaching. A much more secure hypothesis is that the particle ὅτι alerts the reader to a re-presentation of such dialogue or teaching, but does not claim the exact resemblance to which modern minds have become accustomed.

When comparing the accounts of Jesus' healing of the ruler of the synagogue's daughter, we can see that each Synoptic writer gives the most relevant translation or interpretation of this event from the point of view of his audience. Mark will add Aramaic together with a translation:

> καὶ κρατήσας τῆς χειρὸς τοῦ παιδίου λέγει αὐτῇ· ταλιθα κουμ, ὅ ἐστιν μεθερμηνευόμενον·τὸ κοράσιον, σοὶ λέγω, ἔγειρε.
>
> And taking the child's hand he says to her, 'Talitha Koum' which is interpreted as 'Little girl, I am telling you, get up.'

Luke will keep to the Greek:

> αὐτὸς δὲ κρατήσαας τῆς χειρὸς αὐτῆς ἐφώνησεν λέγων·παῖς, ἔγειρε.
>
> But he took her hand and called her saying, 'Child, get up.'

Matthew misses out the direct speech completely:

> εἰσελθὼν ἐκρατήσεν τῆς χειρὸς αὐτῆς, καὶ ἠγέρθη τὸ κοράσιον.
>
> Going in he took her hand and raised the little girl.[2]

1. John 20:18; Acts 1:4-5.
2. Mark 5:41; Luke 8:54; Matthew 9:25.

This is interpretive resemblance, in which a writer selects events and oral records to re-present to others. It is a constant feature of human communication in the present day as in the past. Our current preoccupation with exact resemblance, or an expectation of such, may obscure our understanding of the role of re-presentation, although in oral communication and in relaying information to others we use interpretive resemblance without even thinking about it.

Metaphor

According to RT, the notion of representation is foundational for the understanding of figures of speech such as metaphor and irony, and the latter will be dealt with in detail in Chapter Four. The concept of representation seems to give a more satisfactory account of these tropes than traditional literary analysis. This is based on the notion that when a speaker uses a metaphor, he is loosely resembling his thought or that of someone else. The use of an underdetermined or 'loose' expression may give rise to a wider and richer range of inferences for the hearer than a carefully explicit sentence. Consider the following example from Acts 20:29:

> I know that after my departure fierce wolves will come in to you, not sparing the flock . . .

The figurative language begins earlier, with the believers being considered as a 'flock', but the strong picture language creates a much richer effect than a straight description of false teachers who will cause trouble to the believers in Ephesus.

The speaker may have been representing his thought: *Men will infiltrate the church and destroy it*, but the use of metaphor, viewed in RT as loose resemblance, allows the hearers to draw a much more vivid conclusion and to have a graphic picture of destruction which a literal representation would not have accomplished.[1] It also allows the drawing of inferences about the speaker's attitude to those who will 'come in', namely destructive predators.

Of course metaphor may be misunderstood as a literal utterance, and the passages below show such a misunderstanding,

1. This is explained in much more detail in Noh (2000).

which then came to be used as an accusation. Notice both the 'loose resemblance' to the original as reported in John 2:19 and the explanation of the misunderstanding, which affected even the disciples, given in the following verses (John 2:20-22). I have given the Greek text along with my own translation so that the resemblance may be judged more accurately.

Matthew 26:60:

> ὕστερον δὲ προσελθόντες δύο εἶπαν, Οὗτος ἔφη, Δύναμαι καταλῦσαι τὸν ναὸν τοῦ θεοῦ καὶ διὰ τριῶν ἡμερῶν οἰκοδομῆσαι.
>
> Afterwards two came and said, 'This man said "I am able to destroy the temple of God and to build it again in three days".'

Mark 14:57-58:

> καί τινες ἀναστάντες ἐψευδομαρτύρουν κατ' αὐτοῦ λέγοντες ὅτι Ἡμεῖς ἠκούσαμεν αὐτοῦ λέγοντος ὅτι Ἐγὼ καταλύσω τὸν ναὸν τοῦτον τὸν χειροποίητον καὶ διὰ τριῶν ἡμερῶν ἄλλον ἀχειροποίητον οἰκοδομήσω
>
> Some stood up and gave false witness against him saying, 'We ourselves heard him saying "I will destroy this temple made with hands and in three days I will build another not made with hands."'

Notice the double representation: the writer represents the words of another character who in turn claims to represent the words of Jesus. It is interesting that the actual statement on which such an accusation might have been based does not appear at all in the Synoptic Gospels, which claim to record the words of the false witnesses, but instead in the Gospel of John where there is no mention of such re-presentation by others:

> ἀπεκρίθη Ἰησοῦς καὶ εἶπεν αὐτοῖς, Λύσατε τὸν ναὸν τοῦτον καὶ ἐν τρισὶν ἡμέραις ἐγερῶ αὐτόν.
>
> Jesus responded and said to them, 'Destroy this temple and in three days I will raise it.'[1]

1. John 2:19.

The verses in John's Gospel which follow the original statement explain not only the metaphorical meaning, but also the misunderstanding under which all the hearers laboured and which was resolved for the disciples after the resurrection of Jesus. It seems that it was not understood at all before that. Metaphorical language is rich in contextual implications, but it is significant that this richness was also offset by the deep offence that it caused to the Jews at that time.

The same statement was also echoed by passersby at the time of the crucifixion of Jesus, as reported in Matthew 27:39-40:

> Οἱ δὲ παραπορευόμενοι ἐβλασφήμουν αὐτὸν κινοῦντες τὰς κεφαλὰς αὐτῶν καὶ λέγοντες, ὁ καταλύων τὸν ναὸν καὶ ἐν τρισὶν ἡμέραις οἰκοδομῶν, σῶσον σεαυτόν, εἰ υἱὸς εἶ τοῦ θεοῦ, [καὶ] κατάβηθι ἀπὸ τοῦ σταυροῦ.
>
> And those passing by mocked him, shaking their heads and saying, 'You who destroys the temple and builds it in three days, save yourself if you are the son of God and come down from the cross.'

Here again these passersby were echoing what they *thought* Jesus had said, or what they had heard others report, but their distancing attitude is obvious not only from the words of 'mocking', but also from the body language of 'shaking the head'.

In contrast to this, there is the insistence of the Jewish leaders that the inscription on the cross that Pilate had ordered should be changed to reflect not an actual but a reported state of affairs, as they saw it:

> ἔλεγον οὖν τῷ Πιλάτῳ οἱ ἀρχιερεῖς τῶν Ἰουδαίων, Μὴ γράφε, Ὁ βασιλεὺς τῶν Ἰουδαίων, ἀλλ' ὅτι ἐκεῖνος εἶπεν, Βασιλεύς εἰμι τῶν Ἰουδαίων.
>
> So the Judean chief priests said to Pilate, 'Don't write "The King of the Jews", but that he/that man said, "I am King of the Jews".'[1]

Pilate was happy to insult the Jewish leaders by demonstrating that a crucified man was their king, but the revised wording that the leaders wanted stated a personal claim, albeit a claim that this

1. John 19:21.

writer does not record as ever being made by Jesus. Again, there are three layers of representation in this example.

As a contrast, we have a good example in John 21:23 of speech claimed to be direct and compared with a loose resemblance in order to make a point.

> ἐξ ῆλθεν οὖν οὗτος ὁ λόγος εἰς τοὺς ἀδελφοὺς ὅτι ὁ μαθητὴς ἐκεῖνος οὐκ ἀποθνήσκει οὐκ εἶπεν δὲ αὐτῷ ὁ Ἰησοῦς ὅτι οὐκ ἀποθήσκει ἀλλ ἐὰν αὐτὸν θέλω μένειν ἕως ἔρχομαι [τί πρὸς σέ]?
>
> So the word/report went out to the brothers that that disciple would not die. But Jesus did not say to him 'he will not die' but 'if I wish him to live/remain until I come, what is that to you?'

The common interpretation in biblical studies is that the disciple in question had already died and that this comment on Jesus' words has been added to show that the original was not a prediction.[1] On the other hand, Morris points out that the claim to exact representation in this pericope is unusual for this author:

> In view of the fact that in this Gospel slight variations when statements are repeated are almost universal, it is noteworthy that here the statement is reported exactly from v. 22.[2]

Morris' point is that the author of the fourth Gospel regularly aims for loose rather than exact resemblance, but in the example noted immediately above he is claiming to give a close resemblance. While exact representation is not what the ancients focused on, it appears that writers did attempt to resemble the speech of others as accurately as they could. In either scenario, resemblance rather than identity is all that can be claimed and this is acceptable.

Dealing with Metaphor in Revelation

The book of Revelation raises huge interpretative issues, particularly in relation to what is considered to be literal and what metaphorical. In considering metaphor as 'loose

---

1. Morris, L. (1984 reprint) *The Gospel According to John*. GR, Michigan: Eerdmans, denies that this is a likely scenario, p. 879.
2. Ibid, p. 878-9.

resemblance' to what 'John' saw in a vision, we may be able to remove some of the difficulties with what appear to be polar opposites from a traditional standpoint. If we are able to view expressions such as 'a third of the earth was burned up and a third of the trees were burned up and all the green grass was burned up' as a loose resemblance indicating great destruction, then we are able to deal with the fact of the grass of the earth, plants and trees being spared destruction in the following chapter.[1]

It is important to recognise that, contrary to what we may believe, literalness is *not* normative or privileged.

> If verbal communication were guided by a presumption of literalness, every second utterance would have to be seen as an exception. If it is guided by a presumption of relevance . . . there are no exceptions: the interpretation of every successful act of communication, including utterances in particular, satisfies this criterion.[2]

In other words, we regularly communicate with one another in less than literal language, and so it should come as no surprise that in a literary and even a biblical context loose resemblance is to be expected. Sperber and Wilson give many examples of everyday speech in which we give a relevant, rather than an exact, response to a question about time. If I am asked how long it takes to drive from Glasgow to London I may say '6 hours', but I would be upset if I was accused of lying by someone who had taken 6 and a half hours to complete the journey. Even denoting 'Glasgow' and 'London' is far from exact, but it is relevant, and the estimate of time will also be accepted as relevant.

On the other hand, if I am asked at what time the train leaves for London, then an accurate or literal response such as '9.47am' is more relevant than 'before 10am'. Metaphor, then, is a particular case of loose resemblance which is effective if it is relevant, and will be more powerful in many contexts than a strictly literal representation of a similar proposition.

---

1. Revelation 8:7 followed by 9:4.
2. Wilson and Sperber (2012) *Meaning and Relevance*. Cambridge: CUP, p. 89.

Dealing with Intertextuality or Use of Other Texts by Authors

It will be helpful to separate the different types of intertextuality which are discussed by biblical scholars, particularly in reference to Pauline studies, but also with reference to the book of Revelation. Firstly, in quotations from the Hebrew Bible or Septuagint we may have assumed direct quotation where the words in the new text contain a more or less exact correspondence to the older one. These will almost always be introduced by a formula such as 'it is written', 'Isaiah says', 'as David says', 'Moses says', 'the Scripture says', and so on. Nestle-Aland and United Bible Societies in their respective editions of the Greek text of the NT indicate such a quotation by using a different font. Looking at this category from the perspective of RT, we see that the author is giving a procedural instruction to the readers to process the material as a representation of a text which he accepted as authoritative. It does not follow that his readers would also see it as such, but the strongest inference is that he himself saw it as authoritative and expected his readers would as well.

The book of Romans has around sixty quotations from the Septuagint, and almost all of these are introduced by the formula noted in the previous paragraph, but there are several which are introduced only by the neuter form of the definite article τό.[1] Since these are quotations from the Decalogue, I suggest that this introduction was a sufficient identification of a passage from the Septuagint which was assumed by Paul to be very well-known to his listeners. This usage can be seen also in the Corinthian correspondence.[2]

Now, as stated before, this representation is a 'close' resemblance of the 'original' from an RT perspective. The detailed examination of quoted text that biblical scholars mine in order to discover whether or not the author was using the Hebrew Bible, Septuagint, or a free translation of his own is not relevant when making the point of the communicative intention of the author. We are treating it as a 'close' resemblance in view of the introductory formula which implies this. The use of 'close' here

1. Romans 13:9.
2. 1 Corinthians 4:6 and Galatians 5:14.

does not claim identity but resemblance only. When we come to discuss allusions and nonattributed representations then these will be considered to present a 'loose' resemblance to the original text. The discussion at this point is not about *how* the text is being applied but the form in which it appears.

Secondly, we have quotations that are a partial representation of an earlier text and the question raised by scholars is whether or not the implied author intended the earlier text to be part of his argument. In biblical studies, the use of terms such as 'allusion' and 'echo' have been used to describe references to the Hebrew Bible (or usually Septuagint) that *may* have been part of the communicative intent of the author, or may have been an unconscious inclusion of his own context and world view. Unlike the earlier category of direct quotation, these are not introduced by any overt formula. In particular, 'echo' is used by Richard Hays of material that may be an unconscious usage (re-presentation in RT terms) of utterances found in the earlier texts, while 'allusion' would refer to an *intentional* use of such texts but in indirect form.[1] Such textual reference will be described in this book as 'loose resemblance'. Stanley Porter, on the other hand, considers that 'the notion of echo (can) serve a purpose in describing the indirect introduction of extratextual material into a text.'[2] The context of Porter's statement suggests that 'extratextual' refers to material from a text outside of the one in focus, almost inevitably the Septuagint. It is unfortunate that, by using the term 'indirect', Porter leads his reader to suppose that extratextual material introduced directly is referred to as 'allusion'. To avoid confusion, I intend to use 'direct' and 'indirect' in the normal grammatical way to refer to a quotation that claims to be direct or indirect speech.

The question that such usage seems to raise for biblical scholars is whether or not the implied audience would be able to access such allusions. A further question, of course, is whether or not the writer *intended* them to access them: was this ostensive? By applying the RT concept of representation, we make no claim concerning the hearer's ability to refer to the original context of

1. Hays, R.B. (1989) *Echoes of Scripture in the Letters of Paul.* New Haven: Yale University Press.
2. Porter, S.E. in S.E. Porter and C.D. Stanley (eds.) (2008) *As it is Written: Studying Paul's Use of Scripture.* Atlanta: SBL, pp. 29-40.

the presentation. The author may have such a context in his mind but if he does not make it explicit, then, given that the cultural context and educational background of his listeners differ widely from his own, it is likely that only a subset of hearers will access the original. This does not mean that these hearers would find the communication unintelligible, merely that they would be unable to access the original reference, and the communication would be less successful than it would have been if they shared the author's background: that is, in RT terms, his contextual assumptions and encyclopaedic entries. The communicative intention of the author may not have been as successful as he anticipated, but it has not necessarily failed because his hearers could not identify – at least initially – the source of his allusion. It will still be relevant, but not necessarily in the way in which the writer intended.

Humans make allusions constantly, but only a subset of hearers will access the original. A glance through any serious newspaper will provide many examples of allusions whose original context is unknown to many readers. A recent headline following the 2015 general election in UK stated: 'Miliband and Clegg fall on their swords.'[1] The following paragraph explains this reference, but how many readers cast their minds back to the narrative of Roman generals and their behaviour after suffering defeat in battle? The communication is richer if the reader can access the source, but communication is still successful without it. It is a metaphor in modern terms, but there is also a historical situation in which it was a literal event. As a metaphor, it gives rise to 'more rich cognitive effects' as discussed above, than the bland and literal 'Miliband and Clegg resigned'.

I raise this because the question of readers' or hearers' ability to access the original context of an allusion or quotation has become a source of contention among some scholars. It seems more honest to admit that we simply do not know how many of Paul's audience would have been able to do this. This does not subvert his communicative intention, but merely renders it less 'rich' than it might have been.

The issue of literacy among the Pauline congregations is a major factor in the debate, with Christopher Stanley concluding that most of Paul's congregations would have been illiterate, although

1. *The Guardian* p. 1, 9 May 2015.

this would not have prevented them from deriving meaning from his letters when read out to a congregation.[1] Stanley Porter, on the other hand, offers evidence of a culture that was 'increasingly literate, directly and indirectly', his point being that many people required documents that had to be written, and so they were able to deal with written material even when unable to actually read it for themselves.[2] This question is not germane to the topic here, except to point out that we can 'hear' echoes or allusions from earlier exposure to them even if this has been oral rather than written.

Kathy Ehrensberger has a very helpful perspective on this which sidesteps the issue of whether or not Paul's audience would be able to recognise his allusions – or, indeed, his quotations:

> To refer to the Scriptures thus constitutes not a claim to divine authority on the part of the conversation partners but rather an indication that they perceive themselves as participating in a discourse that is shaped by a perception of life and the world according to the Scriptures, that is according to a Jewish social and symbolic universe.[3]

In other words, Paul was introducing his congregations to such a world view, with many of them being previously unaware of the material quoted or alluded to, but with others there who were able to dialogue with the text.

Re-presenting to Deal with Issues Raised

A further use of re-presentation may appear when an author uses the words of a common belief or well-known saying, sometimes to make a point based on such a common belief, but he assumes

1. Stanley, C. (2012) 'By the end of the seminar, there appeared to be broad agreement that the majority of people in Paul's audiences would have been illiterate and thus incapable of reading the Scripture for themselves, but deep differences remained (among the seminar members) over the implications of this piece of data', in C.D. Stanley (ed.) *Paul and Scripture: Extending the Conversation*. Atlanta: SBL, p. 326.
2. Porter (2008) p. 118.
3. Ehrensberger, K. (2008) 'Paul and the authority of scripture' in S.E. Porter and C.D. Stanley (eds.) *As it is Written: Studying Paul's Use of Scripture*. Atlanta: SBL, p. 310.

that this is understood by his audience. This may be seen in Paul's correspondence with the Corinthian churches, such use now being noted in modern English translations by quotation marks:

> 'All things are lawful for me but not all are profitable.'[1]

The verse following this is also taken by most scholars to be a quotation of a well-known dictum because of the chiasmus which makes it an easily-remembered saying:

> Food for the stomach and the stomach for food.

But the sentiment expressed is not part of Paul's argument. Fee claims it is 'best understood as a Corinthian slogan'.[2] This fits well with Paul's ongoing argument warning against sexual immorality in which he also uses a chiasm to correct the ideas of his hearers:

> The body is not for immorality but for the Lord, and the Lord is for the body.

The difficulty for us which the original readers or hearers of the letter did not have is that we need to be alerted to the fact of such re-presentation. Older English translations did not insert helpful quotation marks, but most recent translations now do this to alert us to the fact that the statement did not originate with Paul. Of course, there is disagreement about the extent of such representation, with many scholars seeing the quotation above running on to the end of the sentence:

> 'Food for the stomach and the stomach for food and God will destroy them both (the stomach and the food).'

I am raising this to show that decisions in such cases are made on pragmatic grounds; namely, the poetic structure of the phrase and its place in the overall argument. Of course, sometimes there are lexical or grammatical signals given to indicate such representation, as for example the phrase 'Now concerning the matters you wrote about', which appears regularly when Paul moves on to a new topic, as in 7:1, 25; 8:1; 12:1 16:1. In 7:1, this introduction leads on directly to the representation of the

1. 1 Corinthians 6:12; 10:23.
2. Fee, Gordon D. (1987) *The First Epistle to the Corinthians*. GR, Michigan: Eerdmans, 1988. p. 254.

issue 'It is good for a man not to touch a woman', which is now recognised not as Paul's belief but as what others believed and which needed to be dealt with. This is not the same as irony, which we will deal with later. This use is dealing with a topic which has already been raised and the words used, or a loose resemblance of them, is re-presented as the apostle deals with it.

A further pointer to a re-presentation of a well-known fact or position is the phrase 'we know that', as is particularly used in chapter 8:[1]

> We know that 'all of us possess knowledge'.
> We know that 'an idol has no real existence'.
> . . . 'there is no God but one.'[2]

The sharing of such knowledge is accepted by Paul, but the hearers are warned that not all share such knowledge.[3] By stating this commonly agreed dictum, the apostle can then build his argument which features the type of 'knowledge' that may be a stumbling block for some of the Corinthians.

Voices Re-presented

Now, the acknowledgement of the use of the words of others by Paul in his letters has led to new theories being put forward suggesting the presence of 'voices' in the letters. Such voices may be of opponents of Paul, or else Paul might be presenting the arguments of others in the manner of the classical diatribe. This is particularly apposite in the case of the letter to the Romans, in which many have discerned features of diatribe. Douglas Campbell's provocative book on this letter, *The Deliverance of God: An Apocalyptic Rereading of Justification in Paul*, suggests that another voice – that of a law-abiding Jew – speaks from

1. This is also a feature found in the *Discourses* of Epictetus 1.9.4.
2. 1 Corinthians 8:1, 4.
3. Scholars disagree about the boundaries marking the position or question of the Corinthians and Paul's own comments. Ciampa, R.E. and Rosner, B.S. (2010) *The First Letter to the Corinthians*. GR, Michigan: Eerdmans, pp. 373-4 point out the lack of agreement over the phrase 'we know that': did Paul say this, or is it part of the Corinthians' question? I have taken it as Paul's introduction to a position known to both sides, but the argument of the passage is not affected by the decision here.

Romans 1:18 to 3:20.[1] He describes this figure as a Jewish male learned figure, the Teacher, who puts forward the standard Jewish understanding of the sinfulness of the Gentiles and the punishment that is coming to them. He relies on the background of the diatribe to support his argument, but I would argue that there may be syntactic clues also in the text. I do not wish to engage with Campbell's argument – the book is around 1,000 pages – and the polemical issues he raises regarding the Western focus on justification, but I note his work here because it is an example of the use of re-presentation to change the perspective of a modern reader, and alert her to the very different presuppositions that Paul's audience would have held. Of course, Campbell is not coming from the perspective of RT, but in essence he is suggesting a re-presentation of the voice of a dialogue partner, and using the concept of cultural context and encyclopaedic knowledge – although he does not describe it in this way – that would have been accessible to the first readers/hearers but not to us.

The danger in attributing beliefs to another 'voice' is that we may not have clear signals that this is a re-presentation, rather than the original thought of the implied author. Campbell delineates six features that were common in diatribe, and also five stylistic indicators that he discerns as present in the passage 1:18-3:20. These features and indicators are not presented as procedural instructions, but they do present pragmatic clues that would have alerted the original readers, although we may be unaware of them.

Campbell points out that the letter would have been read aloud and audiences, as well as readers, were cognisant of the features of προσωποποιία (presentation of argument) and διαφονία (dissonance or opposing view) which were present in a diatribe as arguments went back and forth presenting argument and counter argument, but always spoken by one person. This may be seen clearly in the *Discourses* of Epictetus, where the philosopher goes back and forth between his position and that of an imaginary opponent. The editor of the Loeb edition of this work has added quotation marks to make this clear – even in the Greek text – since modern readers might misunderstand and attribute views to that ancient philosopher which were not his but those of his opponents, the Epicureans.[2] Campbell

1. Campbell, D.A. (2009) *The Deliverance of God: An Apocalyptic Rereading of Justification in Paul.* GR, Michigan: Eerdmans.
2. The first Loeb edition, which has now been reprinted, was in 1928.

also claims that it would have been politic to delay identifying the 'other voice' in the Roman context, since Paul was largely unknown to the recipients. The students of Epictetus, by contrast, would have been in no doubt about the other 'voices'.

I am not convinced of Campbell's argument here, but I do suggest that there may be grammatical signals of dissonance. I give the Greek text of Romans 1:17 and 18 for convenience:

> δικαιοσύνη γὰρ θεοῦ ἐν αὐτῷ ἀποκαλύπτεται ἐκ πίστεως εἰς πίστιν, καθὼς γέγραπται, **ὁ δὲ δίκαιος ἐκ πίστεως ζήσεται**
>
> ἀποκαλύπτεται γὰρ ὀργὴ θεοῦ ἀπ' οὐρανοῦ ἐπὶ πᾶσαν ἀσέβειαν καὶ ἀδικίαν ἀνθρώπων τῶν τὴν ἀλήθειαν ἐν ἀδικίᾳ κατεχόντων
>
> For the righteousness of God is being revealed in it (the gospel) from faith to faith, as it is written 'The just one will live from faith;'
>
> For the anger of God is being revealed from heaven on all impiety and wrongdoing of men who hold back/repress the truth by wrongdoing.

Campbell references Cranfield in a footnote as pointing out that 'an adversative γάρ signals an unexpressed "No" in dialogic text', but in fact J.D. Denniston gives examples of this particle as 'marking the appearance of a new character on the stage'. Now, it is true that in the classical language which was the subject of Denniston's magisterial study, another particle such as ἀλλά would be added, but he also notes that it may introduce an objection and translates 'the point is that' which focuses on γάρ.

In narrative and normal dialogue this particle will support what has gone before, but not necessarily immediately before.[1] In this context 'Yes' might be the most reasonable translation, but although there is no adversative particle accompanying it, the repetition of ἀποκαλύπτεται in verse 18 could be seen as a new view on what was being revealed, particularly since there is a chiasm with the word order reversed:

> δικαιοσύνη γὰρ τοῦ θεοῦ ἐν αὐτῷ ἀποκαλύπτεται . . . (17)
>
> ἀποκαλύπτεται γὰρ ὀργὴ θεοῦ ἀπ' οὐρανοῦ (18)

1. The particle is dealt with in more detail in Chapter Five.

This is not sufficient evidence when taken alone, but when added to Campbell's points noted above it is certainly supporting syntactic evidence.

Lucy Peppiatt on the Corinthian Letters

Lucy Peppiatt also has made a strong argument for Paul's use of rhetorical approaches in his correspondence with the churches in Corinth. It is widely recognised, as we have discussed earlier in this chapter, that Paul does present the questions and opinions of some Corinthians before giving his own views on a topic.

> I explore the possibility that within 11:2-16, 14:20-25 and 14:33b-36 there are Corinthian ideas, expressions and theology that have been incorporated and woven into the text among Paul's own ideas, expressions and theology, and that Paul has done this in such a way as to construct powerful Pauline arguments *against* the Corinthian practices of head coverings for women, speaking in tongues all at once, and banning married women from speaking out in worship services.[1]

Peppiatt suggests, after a careful examination of the problem sections, that it was the men rather than the women in Corinth who were creating a problem by insisting on certain restrictions being placed on those who could take part in worship and the way in which women dressed, both in terms of hair length and hair covering. In order to substantiate this argument, she proposes that 1 Corinthians 11:4-5 is the voice of men in Corinth, as are verses 7-10 of the same chapter. The verses following would then be Paul's exclamation at such a position.

Peppiatt examines the presuppositions that we have come to accept without question, such as the 'problem' of women, but points out that the passages that seem so difficult to reconcile with other Pauline letters would fit in perfectly if attributed to troublesome males in the congregations! Her reconstruction using rhetorical strategies is compelling but I raise it here merely to point out that as well as this, RT gives a theoretical basis for the human propensity to re-present, frequently without acknowledging

1. Peppiatt, L. (2015) *Women and Worship at Corinth*. Eugene, OR: Wipf and Stock, pp. 4-5.

such re-presentation. In addition, RT's acknowledgment of the contribution made by encyclopaedic information and contextual or cultural background to the recovery of implicatures and the derivation of inferences gives a stronger basis for a different reading, but such implicatures and inferences do need to be brought out and examined. The use of diatribe and the extent of its acceptance outside of philosophical schools is part of that encyclopaedic information.

Conclusion

In this chapter we have examined the universal human capacity for re-presenting not only our own thoughts but those of others, frequently with no acknowledgment or even awareness of such representation. As we listen to news broadcasts or read newspapers we cannot help being aware of this, and of the assumption of a shared body of knowledge that makes the communication richer. If there is no body of shared knowledge, then the communication may still be successful, it may achieve relevance, but it will not be so rich. In reading an ancient text we struggle to access such a body of shared knowledge, but recent work in the world of the New Testament on the use of diatribe to effect a powerful argument has brought such knowledge much closer. The understanding that literalness is not normative opens the way for an acceptance of all utterance as 'close' or 'loose' resemblance, and a new appreciation of the role of metaphor, as well as echo and allusion, is an important insight in interpreting the communicative intention of an author or text.

Chapter 4
Verbal Irony

In the previous chapter, we acknowledged that a great deal of our interaction with one another, both orally and in text, contains re-presentations of our thoughts or words or those of others. These re-presentations resemble the original thought either closely or loosely, and we deal with them in a variety of ways. We may claim a close resemblance by using direct speech, although informally, speakers are seldom concerned with giving an accurate representation of another speaker, giving rather a paraphrase of the words spoken. In academic circles, however, 'resemblance' may be seen as an abdication of accuracy, but in fact only the 'thinker' knows the exact form of his thought. Once that thought becomes public in words, it is only a resemblance, although this may be a very close resemblance.

In this chapter, I will deal with the presence of re-presentations with which the writer does not agree.[1] This I will call 'irony'. Although traditionally verbal irony has been classified as a trope or figure of speech, the identification of a particular statement as ironic is fraught with difficulty. It should be noted, however, that verbal irony differs from situational irony, although the two are regularly confused by many, including some biblical scholars.[2] Major works on irony deal with situations which are not what they seem, or, more frequently, in which the reader or hearer knows that the participants in dialogue or action are unaware of factors known to a later reading audience. The topic of this chapter is verbal irony: in RT terms, that is an utterance

1. As discussed in Chapter Three.
2. In contrast to this, Mark Nanos delineates three separate types of irony, but does not deal with verbal irony in *The Irony of Galatians*. Minneapolis: Fortress, 2002, pp. 34.

or representation with which the speaker disagrees, but which is believed by his hearers or other participants. It is an echo of the thought (expressed or otherwise) of another.

In oral communication, there may be body language, the use of a particular intonation or regional accent which gives the hearer a clue to the fact that the speaker is using words ironically, but in written text there is usually no such clue. Even the traditional definition of irony as 'a figure of speech which communicates the opposite of what was literally said' is now being questioned. As noted above, RT proposes a new approach in which irony is defined as *an echoic utterance from which the speaker distances himself.*

This is a widely used trope in political satire. A statement of Prime Minister David Cameron in response to objections to 'austerity' was 'We're all in this together'. This was widely parodied by cartoonists and others who objected to such a statement but then added 'Not!' to indicate such disagreement.[1]

A recent edition of the *Short List* magazine contained an article about Denzel Washington in which the latter recounted his experience when using irony which was not recognised by his hearer. While on a radio phone-in show he was asked the question, 'Would you play James Bond?' He jokingly said, 'Yes, why not? Get out there and start a campaign! Denzel for James Bond!' Unfortunately, his humour was not understood and his words appeared in print as 'We start the Denzel is Bond campaign today!' followed by news stories with the heading 'Denzel desperate to play Bond!' The story was related by Denzel Washington to show the power of online communication and what can happen to information when it is re-presented to a new audience without the understanding of his use of irony.

It is the fact that there is no linguistic marker to introduce irony which makes its identification so difficult. The playwright Tom Stoppard is quoted as saying that there should be a typeface for irony since readers so often fail to recognise it and

1. This is the only particle or lexical item I have found in English to indicate the presence of irony and is used mainly in colloquial settings such as cartoons and advertisements. 'As if' following an ironic utterance would be another marker added in oral, but not written, communication.

thereby either misunderstand the speaker's words or regard him as a liar![1] The need for irony to be recognised is obvious: if we attribute to a speaker thoughts or opinions that he does *not* hold then we are misrepresenting him, and in biblical text this is very serious. It has been said by some who are nervous about attributing an ironic statement to biblical authors that such attribution is an attempt to get out of 'hard' sayings. In response, I would claim that the sayings are 'hard' because we do *not* recognise the speaker's disassociating himself from such an opinion.[2]

In this chapter, the following criteria will be adduced in support of each example:

- Is there evidence that the speaker believes the statement he is uttering?
- Can we identify whose thought or utterance the speaker is echoing?
- Does the context give clues for such identification *or* is there a small syntactic signal in the form of a particle which alerts a discerning hearer? For example the word 'like' in modern colloquial English may function in this way: 'I'm like: I don't know this?'

The use of such criteria prevents a random identification of irony and gives evidence of both the echo and the disassociation. In the NT, the Corinthian correspondence contains many utterances of Paul that are generally regarded as ironic by biblical scholars, as well as other utterances that are in dispute. I will discuss first of all those passages in which irony is unambiguous before considering disputed passages. The former would include 1 Corinthians 4:8a, and 2 Corinthians 11:19; 12:13; 12:16b, while the latter would include 1 Corinthians 11:19 and 2 Corinthians 8:7. The points noted above will be brought to bear on each passage in turn.

1. This quotation is noted by Ian MacKenzie (2002) *Paradigms of Reading*. Basingstoke: Palgrave Macmillan, p. 220.
2. This is related to, but not the same as, the presentation of the argument of another voice which was discussed in the previous chapter. Diatribe also uses irony but I am distinguishing the two forms because the communicative effect is different.

Examples of Unambiguous Irony

1 Corinthians 4:8

> ἤδη κεκορεσμένοι ἐστέ, ἤδη ἐπλουτήσατε, χωρὶς ἡμῶν ἐβασιλεύσατε
>
> You have enough already, you are rich already, without us you ruled/were kings.[1]

The latter part of the verse shows that Paul does *not* believe this of the spiritual state of the Corinthian believers: 'I wish you did reign so that we also might reign with you.' On the other hand, it is clear that the Corinthians, or at least some of them, *did* believe this. There are many verses that refer to the arrogance of at least some in the church.[2] We can say then that the criteria for the identification of irony as an echoic statement (noted above) have been met: Paul does not believe this statement, but the Corinthians do. Then, using point 3, we can see that the latter part of verse 8 supports this analysis as far as Paul is concerned, while the passages in footnote 2 support the view that others did believe it. One further indication may be the three rhetorical questions of verse 7, which seem to function as challenges to strongly held assumptions on the part of some, in addition to the use of 'puffed up' (φυσιοῦσθε) in verse 6.

English translations such as ESV and NIV mark the irony with an exclamation mark which is a mild indication alerting the reader to interpret some astonishment on the part of the speaker. NIV also translates the emphatic particle γε as 'really': 'How I wish you really had become kings!' NLT, however, make the attribution of the thought clearer by adding 'You think you already have everything! You are already rich!' However, there is a question raised by this latter translation: what inferences are lost by making the irony an explicit echo of the Corinthians' ideas? The fact of the disassociation is clear, but the force of the irony is lessened. On the other hand, there is no danger of a reader assuming that Paul believes the statement.

Following on from verse 8 are other statements in verse 10 which may be seen as reflecting the views of the Corinthians about

1. The translations given after the direct quotation of a verse in Greek are my own, but other translations are acknowledged.
2. 1 Corinthians 5:2, 6.

Paul, rather than giving the apostle's own opinion. The grammar is condensed, heightening the contrast between 'we' and 'you':

> ἡμεῖς μωροὶ διὰ Χριστόν, ὑμεῖς δὲ φρόνιμοι ἐν Χριστῷ· ἡμεῖς ἀσθενεῖς, ὑμεῖς δὲ ἰσχυροί· ὑμεῖς ἔνδοξοι, ἡμεῖς δὲ ἄτιμοι
>
> We are foolish because of Christ, but you are wise in Christ; we are weak, but you are strong; you are held in honour, but we are dishonoured.[1]

Some commentators such as Fee[2] and Barrett[3] acknowledge this while others see it as a fact that Paul did believe.[4] NIV and NLT again mark the irony with an exclamation mark, but ESV does not. The issue here is whether or not Paul is stating something that he believes or something that the Corinthians believe. This verse in particular has a strong contrast between 'us' and 'you' the point of which is unclear if irony is not being employed. Since Paul has been disputing the 'wisdom' of the recipients of his letter from the first chapter, it seems unlikely that he's now changing his mind! Furthermore, in verse 14 Paul says, 'I am not writing this to make you ashamed, but to warn you.' I suggest that Paul used irony in these verses to create at least unease – if not shame – among some of the Corinthian believers. This contrast between the opinion of the Corinthians about themselves as Paul portrays it, and their opinion of Paul, is also prominent in the second letter, as we will discuss next.

2 Corinthians 11:19

> ἡδέως γὰρ ἀνέχεσθε τῶν ἀφρόνων φρόνιμοι ὄντες·ἀνέχεσθε γὰρ εἴ τις ὑμᾶς καταδουλοῖ, εἴ τις κατεσθίει, εἴ τις λαμβάνει, εἴ τις ἐπαίρεται, εἴ τις εἰς πρόσωπον ὑμᾶς δέρει. κατὰ ἀτιμίαν λέγω, ὡς ὅτι ἡμεῖς ἠσθενήκαμεν.

---

1. 1 Corinthians 4:10.
2. Fee (1988) 'Paul sets the Corinthians and himself . . . in bold relief, again with total irony', p. 176.
3. Barrett, C.K. (1968) *The First Epistle to the Corinthians.* Peabody, Massachusetts: Hendrickson, 1987. 'The irony of this verse is more subtle than that of verses 8, 9; and the more devastating,' p. 111.
4. Theissen, G. (1982) *The Social Setting of Pauline Christianity.* Edinburgh: T & T Clark.

> For you gladly bear with fools/foolish people since you are (so) wise! Indeed you put up with it if anyone enslaves you, if anyone devours you, if anyone takes (from you), if anyone puts on airs, if anyone hits you in the face. I say in shame, we have been weak!

There are so many assumptions in these verses that we must lay them out in the first instance before attempting to unpack the irony. As was mentioned above, one major issue in the Corinthian correspondence is the issue of 'wisdom', whether worldly or spiritual, and Paul's attitude to the arrogance of the believers in Corinth on account of their veneration of 'wisdom'.

This section begins with the issue of wisdom and foolishness, and with the apostle challenging his hearers to face the issue of whether or not he *was* foolish. There is no evidence to suggest that they did think him foolish, but they did find plenty to criticise. By showing 'boasting' to be foolish, he leaves his auditors to draw the conclusion that others in their midst who were currently boasting might also be held to be 'foolish'.

Paul did *not* think that the Corinthians were wise. The English translations put an exclamation mark after 'wise' to indicate this. NLT again has 'you who think you are so wise' which does show Paul's distancing himself from the statement, but loses the effect of the irony. He states that they are wise, but then in a series of statements which almost certainly reflect what had been happening in their churches, he shows that they have put up with the kind of behaviour that only fools would tolerate.

The final sentence 'we have been weak' is introduced by ὡς ὅτι which is said to be 'an amplified or strengthened form of declarative ὅτι'.[1] This may be taken in different ways. Thrall translates: 'As you say, we have been weak.'[2] This takes the ὅτι as introducing a thought or speech of the Corinthians. Furnish, by contrast, takes the whole phrase as dependent on λέγω and as giving Paul's ironic comment: 'we seem to have been weak' – which of course we are claiming *does* reflect the Corinthians'

1. Jannaris, A.N. (1899) *Historical Greek Grammar.* London: MacMillan & Co., p. 147. Note the use of the same phrase in 2 Corinthians 5:19 and 2 Thessalonians 2:2.
2. Thrall, M.E. (2000) *The Second Epistle to the Corinthians 8-13.* London: T. & T. Clark, p. 718.

views.[1] Furnish also points out that the wider situational irony is that Paul's 'weakness' is in fact 'his greatest boast'.[2] This links with 12:10 and relates to the example following in 12:13.

2 Corinthians 12:13

> τί γάρ ἐστιν ὃ ἡσσώθητε ὑπὲρ τὰς λοιπὰς ἐκκλησίας, εἰ μὴ ὅτι αὐτος ἐγὼ οὐ κατενάρκησα ὑμῶν; χαρίσασθε μοι τὴν ἀδικίαν ταύτην.
>
> So how did you lose out among (beyond) the other churches apart from the fact that I did not burden you? Forgive me this wrong!

It is clear that not only Paul, but any rational observer, would see that a burden is not a gain but a loss. Paul does not believe that he has done wrong, but others seem to believe this as seen in 11:7.[3] The earlier dialogue has suggested that although Paul had the right to claim support from the churches to which he ministered, usually he chose to be independent and to meet his own needs.[4] This careful behaviour, however, seems to have been misinterpreted to suggest that Paul was not a 'true' apostle, the reasoning being that a true apostle would have claimed support. This is the background to his ironic statement. Thrall and Furnish see irony here, as does Barnett. Again, the English translations all treat this as ironic by the insertion of an exclamation mark, leaving the contradiction of 'wrong' and 'not burdening' to supply the distancing. To his opponents, Paul will always be in the wrong, even when refusing to burden the churches by refusing (or more probably not claiming) support from them.

Witherington suggests that in refusing financial help from the Corinthians, Paul was unwilling to accept their patronage, and that this was the real or perhaps underlying issue since the

---

1. Furnish, V.P. (1984) *II Corinthians* AB 32A. New York: Fortress, p. 497-8.
2. Ibid, p. 512.
3. Again in 11:7 a rhetorical question is bringing to the fore the criticism of Paul for not accepting financial help from the Corinthian church: 'Did I commit a sin in humbling myself/because I humbled myself so that you might/should be raised up because/in that I preached the good news of God to you freely?'
4. 1 Corinthians 9:3-15, 18; 2 Corinthians 11:9.

patron/client relationship implied mutuality of some sort.[1] It is not the focus of this chapter, but patronage was a live issue in NT times and should be borne in mind when we examine the context of several of the Pauline epistles. It may also be relevant to the next example.

2 Corinthians 12:16b

ἔστω δὲ, ἐγὼ οὐ κατεβάρησα ὑμᾶς·ἀλλὰ ὑπάρχων πανοῦργος δόλῳ ὑμᾶς ἔλαβον.

Let it be, I didn't burden you; but being/because I was crafty I captured you by guile!

The previous argument continues with Paul raising another complaint that some seem to have made. It is possible that the 'craftiness' in question, particularly in connection with the 'not burdening', refers to the fact that Paul had raised the question of help for the (comparatively) poor believers in Jerusalem. The argument would run like this: you didn't take support from us, but you did 'con' us into making a collection for Jerusalem! From the eighth and ninth chapters it seems that initially the Corinthians were very enthusiastic about helping with support for the believers in Jerusalem, but as the time approached to give the gift they became less eager.[2] The following verses, which talk about Titus and the others who were to take the collection to Jerusalem, support this view.

So, then, Paul does not believe that he is by nature 'crafty' but he knows that others do! Again, the English translations acknowledge this:

ESV: I was crafty, you say.
NLT: They still think I was sneaky . . .
NIV: Crafty fellow that I am, I caught you by trickery!

---

1. Witherington III, Ben (1995) *Conflict and Community in Corinth*. GR, Michigan: Eerdmans, p. 412.
2. Barrett, C.K. (1973) *A Commentary on the Second Epistle to the Corinthians*. Peabody, Massachusetts: Hendrickson. 'Paul has made a great show of asking for no money, but he has instituted what purports to be a collection for the poor saints in Jerusalem, and has pocketed the money himself,' p. 324. Also see Hughes (1986) p. 464.

The translations of ESV and NLT lose the shock element of irony by showing that such a thought was in the minds (or mouths) of the Corinthians rather than being what Paul believed, but they do avoid misunderstanding!

The passages that we have examined so far have all been acknowledged as containing an ironic statement by both commentators and also most of those translating into English. We have shown that Paul distances himself from these statements, but that there is evidence that others did believe them. *Paul echoed what others believed, but distanced himself from that belief.* The context of the examples, both immediate and in the epistle as a whole, support this analysis. Other examples in the Corinthian correspondence are less transparent.

More Contentious Examples of Irony

1 Corinthians 11:19

δεῖ γὰρ καὶ αἱρέσεις ἐν ὑμῖν εἶναι, ἵνα καὶ οἱ δόκιμοι φανεροὶ γένωνται ἐν ὑμῖν.

For it's also necessary that there are divisions among you so that the 'approved' may also become clear among you!

This is a difficult verse because Paul does acknowledge that there is a distinction between those in Corinth who are living as faithful believers and those whose behaviour is a disgrace.[1] The question is, given the context, whether or not that is the point he is making here. Since the subsequent text shows that he does *not* approve of 'divisions' when the believers come together for the Lord's Supper then I suggest that he does *not* want there to be divisions for this celebration, even if in practice there are differences of behaviour in the church. So if Paul does *not* think that there should be a division, whom is he echoing and what is the point he is making with this ironic statement?

One possibility is that he is voicing the thoughts of those who saw themselves as 'well-behaved' and therefore 'approved' (δόκιμοι), in contrast to the sexually immoral. This, however, does not seem to be the basis on which the divisions were made. The remainder of the eleventh chapter deals with the separation of

1. 1 Corinthians 4:18-19; 5:11.

those who 'have' from those who 'don't have', a distinction that is economic or social rather than moral. A more likely possibility is that he was echoing the thoughts of these more affluent believers, who were perhaps taking their favourable economic situation to be the result of God's blessing. They believed that there had to be a separation between those who could show the approval of God in material terms and those who could not.

The following passage begins with the particle οὖν which shows the *result* of such divisions and connects again with συνερχομένων in the previous verse before the ironic utterance. Those who have plenty are eating and drinking – to excess in some cases – and others are going hungry. Finally, in verse 22, he concludes with the rhetorical question 'Shall I praise you?' and gives the clear answer: 'I don't praise (you) in this!' This repeats the introductory 'I don't praise you' in verse 17.

I suggest that the irony in verse 19 sets the scene for Paul's condemnation of the kind of behaviour that makes distinctions between believers on the basis of their economic status. He echoes a feeling held by some at Corinth, while his own conviction is that there should *not* be such a distinction. There is a wider question here regarding the physical situation that pertained when the house churches in Corinth met together. The assumption behind this identification of irony is that there were two potential spaces in which the assembled could eat their meal, one being further within the Roman 'villa' and so more private, and the other nearer the entrance, or even in the garden space in the centre of buildings of that era. This assumption is not necessary for the argument, but if indeed this was the setting, then it supports a physical division as well as a financial one.

Witherington agrees with this 'villa' setting for this chapter and its being a contributing factor to the social divisions, and views this verse as 'expressing mock disbelief' that there can actually be factiousness at this celebration.[1] Horsley, meanwhile, thinks that verse 21 'should also be read as a rhetorical accusation and not as a precise explanation of what is bothering Paul'.[2]

This conclusion, however, does not seem to be supported by older commentators. Fee acknowledges that it *might* be ironic,

1. Witherington (1995) p. 412.
2. Horsley, R.A. (1998) *1 Corinthians*. Nashville: Abingdon Press, p. 159.

but he doesn't think so. Barrett likewise sees the 'divisions' as 'a divine, eschatological necessity', but I do not! This is *not* what the apostle is writing about at this point. Campbell, Fitzmyer, Garland and Thiselton, however, are in no doubt about the irony. Fitzmyer: 'It seems preferable to say that Paul is indicating ironically the reason for his dismay at the dissensions and why he cannot praise the Corinthians.'[1] Campbell understands οἱ δόκιμοι to be 'the dignitaries' and translates:

> For there actually has to be discrimination in your meetings so that, if you please, the elite may stand out from the rest.[2]

I suggest that here the fact of Paul's disagreement with the statement 'there has to be division among you' must be clearly understood as an ironic statement in order to avoid the inference that the apostle supported such division. This verse has been used by certain churches to 'fence' the communion table and prevent those who may be 'unworthy' from participating. It is time to reassess the reasons for unworthiness in the Corinthian context and then in gatherings in the situations of today. In the wider context of the eleventh chapter, Paul writes that his understanding of their situation is that when they come together it is 'not for the better but for the worse'.[3] Surely this indicates that the state of affairs in their gathering (note the repeated use of συνέρχομαι) is not one of which the apostle approves.

2 Corinthians 8:7

> ἀλλ' ὥσπερ ἐν παντὶ περισσεύετε, πίστει καὶ λόγῳ καὶ γνώσει καὶ πάσῃ σπουδῇ καὶ τῇ ἐξ ἡμῶν ἐν ὑμῖν ἀγάπῃ, ἵνα καὶ ἐν ταύτῃ τῃ χάριτι περισσεύητε.
>
> But as you abound in everything: in faith, in word, in knowledge and in all eagerness/enthusiasm and in love from us to you, you should abound in this gracious act also.

The context here is Paul's desire to have a contribution from the Corinthian church to add to the general collection that he was organising for the poor in the Jerusalem church. It is clear from

1. Fitzmyer, J.A. (2008) *First Corinthians.* London: Yale University Press, p. 433.
2. Campbell, NT 33: 61-70.
3. 1 Corinthians 11:17.

verse 10 of this chapter that the Corinthians had originally been very enthusiastic about such a gift, but it seems that as time went on they were dragging their feet in the matter. The whole of the eighth and ninth chapters are dealing with this and urging the Corinthians to 'put their money where their mouth was'. Indeed in verse 13 we have, I suggest, a report of the general feeling about the collection:

> οὐ γὰρ ἵνα ἄλλοις ἄνεσις, ὑμῖν θλῖψις, ἀλλ' ἐξ ἰσότητος
>
> For it should not be 'relief for others, hardship for you' but from equality/being equal.[1]

As I discuss in Chapter Five, the particle ἵνα introduces a potential situation. The lack of a main verb here makes a translation of 'purpose' inappropriate, if not impossible. Rather, the particle indicates what 'should' happen with the Corinthians' opinion of what Paul was asking; namely, 'relief for them and hardship for us', but the negative before it means that Paul is denying such an interpretation.

With this background in mind, I suggest that the first part of 8:7 quoted above reflects not what Paul believed about the Corinthians, but what they thought about themselves. Paul is building his argument on their satisfaction about their own gifts. Since the kind of giving which he was asking for was also a spiritual gift (note use of χάρις here), he is urging them to add to the spiritual gifts they already are so proud of! Of course, it could also be analysed as flattery, but it does reflect the Corinthians' opinion of themselves as noted in 1 Corinthians 1:31; 4:7, and 10.

Unfortunately, no commentators seem to take up this point, perhaps because in 1 Corinthians 1:4-5 he has praised or at least acknowledged their giftedness. It could be seen as a subtle point: Paul is acknowledging their giftedness, or *he is using their own opinion of their giftedness* to make the point that giving is also a spiritual gift to be desired. Paul may also be using the wide scope of χάρις here to refer to both material and non-material gifts. Certainly several scholars have commented on the apostle's use of flattery here to intensify his call for a contribution to the collection. Thrall sees it as a rhetorical ploy to encourage Corinthians to give, while Furnish sees it as an urging to them to increase in a further

1. F.F. Bruce puts it well. 'This criticism of the collection may well have been voiced at Corinth during the recent unpleasantness.' Bruce, F.F. (1971) *1 & 2 Corinthians*. London: Oliphants, p. 223.

spiritual gift. Betz does not identify irony, but he does point out that the last two 'gifts' had not so far been noted among them, namely eagerness and love. The presence of these would be seen in the way the Corinthians dealt with this current request.

> What is implied in Paul's argument is that the last virtue, that of charity, would determine whether they could legitimately claim anything at all, or whether all their claims would be shown to be false.[1]

Here I suggest that the irony or an identification of 'flattery' might also be a relevant reading. It does seem to be the case that Paul is giving lavish praise here for graces that were not immediately evident but which he very much hoped to see displayed in the response to the collection.

Wider Application of This Definition of Irony

The focus of this chapter so far has been on ironic utterances in the Corinthian correspondence, since several of these have already been acknowledged both by commentators and translators, and the point at issue, namely the echoing of another's thought or speech, can be more easily seen. Of course the issue is much wider than this. Just one example from the Hebrew Bible will alert us to the fact that the prophets in particular used irony to great effect. Consider the words of Micaiah ben Imlah in 1 Kings 22:15: 'Attack and be victorious for the Lord will give it into the king's hand', to which Ahab responds: 'How many times must I make you swear to tell me nothing but the truth in the name of the Lord?' There is no overt signal of irony but the king knows that Micaiah is repeating what the other prophets have said in 22:6 and 12, while he himself disagrees with this. Micaiah then gives them his real prophetic utterance: 'I saw all Israel scattered on the hills like sheep without a shepherd . . .' This is a beautiful example of irony being a representation that was not only believed but actually stated, and that the speaker then is echoing while distancing himself from it.

The prophecy of Ezekiel[2] has many examples of biting irony, as has the prophecy of Amos:

1. Betz, H.D. (1985) *2 Corinthians 8 and 9*. Hermeneia. Philadelphia: Fortress Press, p. 59.
2. Ezekiel 20:25, compared with 20:11 and 31. This is the subject of a paper by R.J. Sim.

'Come to Bethel and transgress; to Gilgal and multiply transgression;
Bring your sacrifices every morning your tithes every three days;
Offer a sacrifice of that which is leavened, and proclaim freewill offerings, publish them;
For so you love to do, O people of Israel,' declares the Lord God.[1]

The prophet has indicated that he does *not* want the people to continue to observe the law outwardly at a false shrine while ignoring the ethical demands of the Sinai covenant. This is a representation of the mindset of the people, the use of the phrase 'that which is leavened', and 'so you love to do' giving additional clues to the verbal irony here.

A further example – perhaps a little more contentious – is Jesus' reply to the Canaanite/Syro-Phoenician woman in Matthew 15:26 and Mark 7:27.

> οὐκ ἔστιν καλὸν λαβεῖν τὸν ἄρτον τῶν τέκνων καὶ βαλεῖν τοῖς κυναρίοις
>
> It isn't good to take the children's bread and throw it to the dogs.

This has always been a difficult saying. The context in both Matthew and Mark is a discussion of what is ritually clean or unclean. Following this, Jesus went to the region of Tyre and Sidon, which was an ethnically mixed area. Note further that in both contexts this episode is followed by the healing of the sick and the feeding of the crowd of 4,000. This is generally regarded as being composed of non-Jews, or at least those regarded as being of suspect birth.[2] By recognising that Jesus was echoing common Jewish opinion[3] and, of course, the outlook of his disciples in saying 'It's not good to take the children's bread and throw it to the dogs', we do not attribute to Jesus a saying that seems to

1. Amos 4:4-5.
2. Based on the statement 'they praised the God of Israel'.
3. Wilson (2009) 'Irony and Metarepresentation' *UCL Working Papers in Linguistics* 21 183-226, p. 203 points out that the echoic utterance may not be 'tied to a particular individual, time and place, but is widely entertained or expressed by a certain group of people'.

be contrary to his practice and mission.[1] One only has to look at the theological gymnastics that commentators engage in to see that in taking this literally, rather than as a trope, we seriously misunderstand what was going on.

It is also relevant to note that in the Gospel of Matthew the book ends with a command to go to 'all nations', while the initial sending out of the disciples in the tenth chapter limits their mission to 'the lost sheep of the house of Israel'. I suggest that initially the disciples were not mentally prepared for a wider ministry to other people groups, but that this critical incident (in which Jesus voices their conviction but then acts in opposition to it) was a preparation for the wider command in 28:19.

This chapter is a plea for considering the RT definition of irony as a workable tool for exegetes and translators when faced with statements/utterances that seem to be in conflict with the views of the speaker/writer expressed in other contexts. Of course it can be abused, but failure to recognise irony then attributes to the speaker a belief that he does not hold, while losing the impact of the irony (the reason why he has chosen to utter such a view) on the situation or teaching in question. By using the criteria delineated at the beginning of this chapter, we can make an identification of irony without being accused of the random abandonment of a 'hard' saying. It is also worth noting Clark's comment that 'it is much more common to comment ironically on a state of affairs where things have gone wrong than to comment ironically on a state of affairs where everything has gone right'.[2]

Such rhetorical devices as irony and rhetorical questions can also be found in the writings of the Stoic philosopher Epictetus who, like Paul, made powerful use of diatribe to carry his point. This is seen in particular in the way in which both men re-present other opinion or summon other voices in support of their argument. It should also be remembered that Paul's letters would almost certainly have been read aloud, most probably by the bearer of the letter, to an assembled gathering, rather than being perused individually as we do now.

It is also worth considering the effect of irony both in our modern world and in that of the Middle East in the first century.

---

1. Luke 7:1-10, 9:51-55, 10:33-36.
2. Clark (2013) p. 291.

Shame and honour were inescapable factors in first century society and, as demonstrated below in the dialogues of Epictetus, quoting supposed opinions with a distancing attitude could create shame in a way that a straight statement would not. It was and still is a very effective trope.

The use of ironic statement by Epictetus in his *Discourses* supports what I have claimed for the Pauline letters above. Intriguingly, one example is very similar to Jesus' comment on the way in which some Pharisees avoided helping their parents while adhering to tradition:

> **καλὸς συμπότης** καὶ σύνδειπνος Σωκρατικός
>
> A fine dining companion you would be for Socrates![1]
>
> καὶ ἔλεγεν αὐτοῖς· **καλῶς ἀθετεῖτε** τὴν ἐντολὴν τοῦ θεοῦ, ἵνα τὴν παράδοσιν ὑμῶν στήσητε.
>
> He said to them, 'You have set aside the command of God well, that you might keep your tradition!'[2]

The insertion of an exclamation mark makes the reader aware that the speaker might not think that the statement preceding it is 'good', but it is the context that would give a hearer the best clue to the 'echo'. Both the gluttonous feasters parodied by Epictetus and the zealous Pharisees addressed by Jesus *did* think that their behaviour was acceptable. By echoing such a view but with a distancing attitude which would be clear from the context the condemnation is much stronger and more vivid than a mere statement.

Epictetus has a much longer ironic presentation in 2.20.22-26 in which he inveighs against the Epicureans by putting into their mouths what he claims they are teaching and then finishing with his own 'Well done, philosopher!' This is a short extract from the translation of W.A. Oldfather:

> 'The gods do not exist, and even if they do, they pay no attention to men, nor have we any fellowship with them, and hence this piety and sanctity which the multitude talk about is a lie told by imposters and sophists, or, I swear, by legislators to frighten and restrain evildoers.' Well done, philosopher!

1. *Discourses* 2.4.8.
2. Mark 7:9.

> You have conferred a service upon our citizens, you have recovered our young men who were already inclining to despise things divine.[1]

The Epicureans may have thought that they were rendering a service to society, but Epictetus certainly did not believe that and goes on to suggest ironically that all the wonderful deeds achieved in the history of Greece, from Thermopylae to the actions of the Athenians when facing the Persians, had arisen as a result of such philosophy.

Epictetus' rhetoric was powerful because he used irony to present the beliefs of his opponents as if he agreed with them, but in the act of so doing he exposed such beliefs as incongruent with good living and the principles of Greek society. The editors of the Loeb edition of the *Discourses* have added quotation marks to ironic statements and exclamation marks to the response of Epictetus both in the Greek text and the translation. This of course makes it clear that he is putting words into his opponent's mouth, and so avoids any misunderstanding, but the original oral presentation would not have such aids. The hearers would be faced with an apparently aberrant statement proceeding from the mouth of the master. They would then be shocked into considering this and then rejecting the propositions as echoes of a deviant view. I suggest also that the use of verbal irony by Epictetus supports the argument set out in this chapter.

The function of a rhetorical question is frequently very similar to that of an ironic statement: the question brings to the fore what some of the auditors may think or believe and by questioning that, the speaker is able to refute it, without directly attributing the thought to anyone. This was frequently used not only by orators in the Greco-Roman world but also by Stoic philosophers such as Epictetus, his *Discourses* giving strong resonances to the style of the Pauline epistles.[2] Rhetorical questions, however, merely present that other opinion as a question; the hearer has to give an answer to herself at least, whereas the use of irony seems to bring in the element of shame and ridicule which creates a powerful dynamic.

---

1. *Discourses* 2.20.22-23.
2. The *Discourses* have a considerable number of examples of verbal irony, many of which have been marked by the editor with exclamation marks. 2.4.8 and 2.20.26 are good examples.

Conclusion

We have argued that the RT definition of irony as echoing a thought, belief or utterance of another while maintaining a distancing attitude to such an utterance is an extremely useful one, in that it enables us to avoid attributing to a speaker or writer a belief to which he did not ascribe. Furthermore, the powerful effect of this trope will not be lost. Some scholars have been nervous about the identification of this trope, as noted above, but if we can see it so clearly in the prophets of ancient Israel, it is highly probable that later generations used it also, and the works of Epictetus support this.

Chapter 5
Small Words that Guide Interpretation

In Chapter Two, we considered the way in which a reader or hearer may expect a relevant communication, and the mechanisms many languages have to guide a reader from understanding the communication in a way that the speaker would not have intended. This chapter deals with the way in which a speaker of Koine guided a hearer to interpret his communicative intention. The chapter will be more of a stretch for those who have no knowledge of Greek, but the principles involved seem to be universal. English has particles that guide hearers, and volumes have been written about the contribution to relevance of the particles 'like', 'but', 'as', 'indeed', and others.

There are some small words in Greek that are very helpful guides in interpreting the phrases or clauses that they introduce. Traditionally, they have been read as if they have a fixed lexical meaning, and this has led to some difficult translations both logically and theologically, in which a theological agenda has been pinned on a fixed lexical meaning that the language cannot sustain. Relevance theory deals with such words as giving *procedural instructions* to a reader or hearer to process the following phrase, clause or sentence in a certain way. In other words, it constrains the range of possible meanings and gives clues to the reader about the communicative intention of the author. The assumption is that these are present in the text to make something ostensive.[1]

Some properties that may help to identify a candidate for marking procedural meaning have been suggested as follows:

1. Chapter Two deals with the concept of ostension and a speaker's intention to communicate.

they are difficult to paraphrase, or difficult to translate; they lack synonymous conceptual counterparts. Billy Clark helpfully suggests a basic criterion for such a decision:

> a procedural analysis is justified when it provides the best available account of how a particular expression is understood.[1]

These particles seem to indicate the way in which the phrase or sentence they introduce might be relevant. This in turn helps the reader or hearer to process better the text that they introduce, and so make the communication more salient for her.

This chapter does not attempt to give an exhaustive list of such particles in Koine and the procedural instructions I suggest they encode, but it will examine some of the most relevant for exegesis.

ἵνα, ὅτι, ὡς, καίπερ, εὐθύς, γάρ and οὖν are the particles we will deal with as procedural markers to guide interpretation.

῞Ινα as Introducing a Re-presentation

The particle ἵνα in Greek is the most critical of these small words. It has been viewed as introducing a clause of 'purpose', and as such has been assigned the meaning 'in order that'.[2] There is no doubt that some of the clauses that it introduces do express purpose, but we must consider the wider function of this little word in order to be both faithful to the language of the writers of the New Testament and, more importantly, to avoid attributing to them an intention or purpose they would never have considered. Those examples in which the particle introduces purpose should be decided on the basis of the context, and not the presuppositions of the reader.

Let's consider a well-known verse in 1 John 1:9, which contains this small particle:

> ἐὰν ὁμολογῶμεν τὰς ἁμαρτίας ἡμῶν, πιστὸς ἐστιν καὶ δίκαιος **ἵνα** ἀφῇ ἡμῖν τὰς ἁμαρτίας καὶ καθαρίσῃ ἡμᾶς ἀπὸ πάσης ἀδικίας.
>
> If we confess our sins he is faithful and just **in that** he should forgive our sins and cleanse us from all wrongdoing.

1. Clark (2013) p. 323.
2. This has been dealt with in much more detail in Sim, M.G. (2011) *Marking Thought and Talk in New Testament Greek*. Cambridge: James Clarke & Co.

If we persist in believing that ἵνα means 'in order that', then we are faced with a statement that God is faithful and just in order that he may forgive our sins. No one believes that! Rather, God's forgiveness of human sin is grounded in his faithfulness and justice. The little word ἵνα introduces us to a re-presentation of the thought or intention of the subject: *he must forgive our sins and cleanse us from all wrongdoing*. This example is fairly straightforward and may help us to work through more difficult examples below.

In the Gospel of John 9:2-3, the disciples in the context of seeing a man who had been blind since birth are presented as asking, 'Rabbi, who sinned – this man or his parents, that he was born blind?'

> Ῥαββί, τίς ἥμαρτεν, οὗτος ἢ οἱ γονεῖς αὐτοῦ, ἵνα τυφλὸς γεννηθῇ;
>
> Rabbi, who sinned, this man or his parents, that he was born blind?

They seem to have been articulating the common Jewish[1] belief of that time that disability was the result of sin.[2] They were then asking Jesus to identify the immediate agent of 'sin' – the man (in the womb) or his parents. It is also possible that, more daringly, they were testing this view on Jesus. If we take the ἵνα clause as indicating purpose then we are faced with a logical impossibility, that the man or his parents sinned in order that he might be born blind. Since this seems to be impossible, commentators on the whole have rejected this, but have suggested in its place a result clause: 'so that he was born blind'. This is possible, since there are examples in post-Classical Greek of this particle introducing a wide range of clause types, but based on what we have been proposing in earlier chapters I suggest a clearer way.

This particle introduces a re-presentation of a view commonly held: *he had to be born blind*. This then preserves the context in which disability was seen as proceeding from 'sin' of one kind or another and leads very neatly into Jesus' response in the following verse:

1. Babylonian Talmud *Shabbath* 55a.
2. Schnackenburg, R. (1982) *The Gospel According to St John* Vols. 1-3. New York: Crossroads, p. 240, 'an ancient and oppressive question has been given a new answer by Jesus'.

> ἀπεκρίθη Ἰησοῦς, Οὔτε οὗτος ἥμαρτεν οὔτε οἱ γονεῖς αὐτοῦ, ἀλλ' ἵνα φανερωθῇ τὰ ἔργα τοῦ θεοῦ ἐν αὐτῷ.
>
> Jesus replied, 'Neither this man sinned nor his parents, but the works of God must/should be revealed in him.'

The response goes on:

> ἡμᾶς δεῖ ἐργάζεσθαι τὰ ἔργα τοῦ πέμψαντός με ἕως ἡμέρα ἐστιν.
>
> 'We must do the work of the one who sent me while it is day.'

The aspect of necessity that the ἵνα clause introduces is continued by the use of δεῖ in the following sentence. The issue is not that the man 'must' be born blind, but that in the purpose of God light 'must' come. That is the inevitability, not the sin of the parents. In John 9:3, then, the elliptical comment of Jesus, 'Neither this man sinned nor his parents', denies the link between sin and disability rather than proclaiming their sinlessness, and leads on to the real point in the pericope, which is the healing of this blind man, and in the wider picture to the bringing of light to the world.

From the text above, we can see that the clause introduced by 'but' is immediately followed by the particle ἵνα, but there is no 'main clause' to which this ἵνα clause could be subordinated. In other words, the ἵνα clause *is* the main clause. For many older scholars, however, as well as many translators, this proved unacceptable and an ellipsis was posited such as 'this happened . . .' With such an ellipsis, the particle could still be 'translated' as 'in order that', making the man's blindness a deliberate action of God in order to show his glory. We are then bound into the picture of a God who causes blindness so that his works can be shown many years later. Since the whole pericope deals with the bringing of light and Jesus as 'light of the world', such an interpretation seems obtuse as well as grammatically inept.

Mark 4:12

> Καὶ ἔλεγεν αὐτοῖς, Ὑμῖν τὸ μυστήριον δέδοται τῆς βασιλείας τοῦ θεοῦ, ἐκείνοις δὲ τοῖς ἔξω ἐν παραβολαῖς τὰ πάντα γίνεται, ἵνα βλέποντες βλέπωσιν καὶ μὴ ἴδωσιν, καὶ ἀκούοντες ἀκούωσιν καὶ μὴ συνιῶσιν, μήποτε ἐπιστρέψωσιν καὶ ἀφεθῇ αὐτοῖς.

> And he said to them, 'It is to you that the secret of the kingdom of God has been given but to those outside everything is in parables that while looking they see but do not perceive and while listening they hear but do not understand lest they turn and I forgive them.'

The issue of the harshness of this verse has caused much debate, and has prompted the articulation of the 'parable theory' in order to explain the seeming contradiction in the use of a teaching method designed to elucidate, but apparently used to obfuscate. Vincent Taylor comments:

> This interpretation of the parables is so intolerable that from earliest times it has been questioned.[1]

Taylor's comment reflects earlier scholarship but more recent scholars such as Räisänen and Marcus suggest that the Marcan community may have required the comfort of knowing that, although suffering persecution, they were 'insiders' to whom secrets had been revealed. The parable theory consists of two elements.[2] On the one hand, there is sharp division between disciples and people in general; and, on the other, there is a view of the incomprehensible nature of the parables and their aim of hardening others.[3] Räisänen does point out the tensions in this theory, particularly in Mark 8:17 where the disciples are challenged about their 'hardened' hearts – something which should not have happened to them, but to those 'outside'. Marcus, however, would disagree with suggestions of inconsistency, in that 'all Marcan parables have *some sort* of explanation', even if this is contextual rather than an overt interpretation, as in the parable of the sower.

The example of the hardening of Pharaoh's heart, and of those who are opposed to God or God's people, is often quoted to support a purposive reading of ἵνα in this section.[4] The inference

1. Taylor, V. (1959) *Gospel According to St Mark*. London: MacMillan & Co., p. 257.
2. See further comments below.
3. Räisänen, H. (1990) *The 'Messianic Secret' in Mark's Gospel*. Edinburgh: T. & T. Clark, p. 87
4. Particularly Evans, C. (1989) *To See and Not Perceive: Isaiah 6:9-10 in Early Jewish and Christian Interpretation*. JSOTSup 64. Sheffield: JSOT pp. 96-7, but also Marcus, J. (2005) *Mark 1-8*. London: Doubleday, p. 253 and p. 306.

then is that God will deliberately prevent 'those outside' from hearing or seeing in a meaningful way. The context of this passage, however, is related rather to a deliberate refusal by the religious leaders to acknowledge that the miracles performed by Jesus were done in the power of God. The following sections reiterate the fact of parabolic teaching and the purpose of the coming of the light which is *not* to be hidden, but to be revealed.[1]

If we can suspend our conviction that ἵνα signals a purpose clause, then we will have a clearer view of the function of this particle in introducing the Isaianic quotation in Mark 4:12. After all, the crux of the difficulty is the apparent statement that the *purpose* of the parables is that those listening should not see, hear, understand, repent, nor be forgiven. It seems to be a fact that the listeners did not always understand, and that the disciples were prominent among this group.

To return to the quote from Isaiah: the context there is clearly *not* literal but figurative speech. The prophecies before and after indicate clearly that the prophet's work was to recall the people to follow the Lord their God, not to hinder that process. The people had 'heard' and 'seen' for many years, but they had not changed their ways. The passage in effect presents in poetic form both the present state of the nation and the result of the prophet's work. When the author presents Jesus as quoting this prophecy, he is inviting his readers to draw the same contextual effects as the hearers of the original prophecy, that there will always be observers and hearers who do not understand the significance of what they have seen and heard.[2] The use of the ἵνα clause guides the reader to expect a re-presentation. In this context, it seems to be a re-presentation of what the prophet Isaiah 'said', ironically in a similar context of disbelief.[3] If we wish to infer purpose from this clause, we must find it in the context, not in the use of the particle ἵνα. I believe that the notion of purpose is lacking from that context, in that it is far from proved that the purpose of Jesus was to hinder his hearers from understanding.

1. Mark 4:21-25; 33-35.
2. Marcus (2005) does note that '"those outside" are . . . Jesus' opponents, people who have deliberately excluded themselves from the circle of salvation by their attitude of hostility to Jesus', p. 306.
3. On the parallel passage in Luke: 8:10 we may note the comments of I.H. Marshall (1978) *The Gospel of Luke*. Exeter: Paternoster, and J. Nolland which are not substantially different, although not employing RT terminology.

Several scholars have linked ἵνα and a 'purpose' interpretation of the particle to the use of μήποτε in the quotation, but the latter is *part* of the quotation whereas the former introduces it.[1] If the particle is taken as giving procedural instructions to expect a re-presentation, then the burden of proving whether or not this representation indicates purpose, potential result or a recollection of an earlier prophetic statement is left to the judgement of the reader.[2] The context and encyclopaedic information available to her will lead her to a decision, not any dictionary meaning of the particle.

The 'Parable Theory': Insiders and Outsiders

Watson links the secrecy motifs to a doctrine of predestination including the deliberate hiddenness of the parables:

> By breaking the earlier connection between the parable and its interpretation in this way, Mark emphatically asserts the view that was already present in the tradition: true understanding is given only to the disciples.[3]

The fact that there are two groups, however, does not necessitate the parables being used to exclude and this is the point of my argument.[4] Joel Marcus also focuses on the Marcan

---

1. I disagree with Räisänen (1990) here: 'The meaning of μήποτε is determined by the ἵνα; both conjunctions reinforce each other so that 4:12 has a final meaning from start to finish,' p. 83.
2. See suggestions made by Jannaris (1897); Turner, N. (1963) *A Grammar of New Testament Greek III. Syntax.* Edinburgh: T. & T. Clark; Mandilaras, B. G. (1973) *The Verb in the Greek non-literary papyri.* Athens: Hellenic Ministry of Culture and Sciences; Caragounis, C.C. (2004) *The Development of Greek and the New Testament.* Tübingen: Mohr Siebeck, for the extended use of this particle in Koine. Morna Hooker (1991) notes that 'Jewish thought tended to blur the distinction between purpose and result,' *The Gospel According to St Mark.* London: A. & C. Black, p. 128.
3. Watson, F. (1985) 'The Social Function of Mark's Secrecy Theme'. *JSNT* 7.24, p. 58.
4. Marcus also sees the responsibility for the ability of some to 'hear' and others to misunderstand as resting with God in (1986) *The Mystery of the Kingdom.* SBLDS 90. Atlanta: Scholars Press, p. 90. But Moule (1969) denies any predestinarian overtones, 'Mark 4:1-20 Yet Once More' in E.E. Ellis and M.E. Wilcox (eds.) *Neotestamentica et Semitica: Studies in Honour of Matthew Black*, p. 99.

community, their suffering and their bewilderment on account of the poor reception that the message of Jesus received among Jews in particular, but also among Gentiles. The parable of the sower then explains that although Satan is responsible for the poor reception of some of the seed, there will be a harvest.[1] This is the 'mystery' that has been entrusted to them, but not to those 'outside'. If, however, we can lay aside the conviction of the purposive nature of the ἵνα that introduces verse 12, then we may still view the Marcan community as Marcus does, but without the necessity of 'one of the most formidable sayings in the entire New Testament'. The issue is of God's *intention* that Jesus' parables 'should not enlighten the outsiders but that they should blind them, choke off their understanding and prevent their attainment of repentance and forgiveness'.[2] The parables caused division, but that division was a result of strong resistance to the need for repentance on the part of much of the religious community, a situation that echoed the 'hardness' of the people to whom the prophet preached in an earlier age.[3]

The Isaianic prophecy is also touched on in John's Gospel in the context of unbelief, and although the text says 'they could not believe', this relates to the irony of the original prophecy which, if taken literally, claims that God has hardened their hearts so that he cannot heal them. Nevertheless, the context in John 12:37ff expresses amazement that 'they did not believe' in spite of all the signs done before them, and calling on the experience of the prophet who says, in essence, 'Who's listening to me?' We have to take verbal irony seriously, as we discussed in Chapter Four.

Of course, one may claim that the representation that ἵνα introduces in 4:12 is one of purpose, but that must be supported from the context, and not from some 'intrinsic' meaning of this particle. The verb in the main clause is γέγονεν, the perfect tense of γίνομαι. To support a telic reading of ἵνα in this context, we have to insist on the action in the main clause taking place with the aim of creating the potential result in the subordinate

1. Marcus, J. (1984) 'Mark 4:10-12 and Marcan Epistemology'. JBL 103 557-74, p. 566.
2. Marcus (2005) p. 305.
3. Those who opposed Jesus in the religious community as they heard the parables were described as 'knowing he was talking about them' in Matthew 21:45; Mark 12:12; and Luke 20:19.

clause. This is not possible with the verb 'to be' and it seems unlikely, although not impossible, with an antecedent verb γίνομαι. It seems more reasonable to argue that 'everything is/happens in parables' is a statement of fact then followed by an ironic quotation which applied to the situation of Jesus' audience as it did to Isaiah's centuries before. I submit that the criteria for identifying the quotation as a subordinate clause reflecting the *purpose* of the parables are not present.

It is significant that in Luke's account of this interaction with the Isaianic prophecy in 8:10 only the first part of Isaiah 6:9 is quoted, with the remaining portion appearing in Acts 28:26-27 in the context of Jewish leaders disagreeing with Paul about Jesus and Paul's response: 'God's salvation has been sent to the Gentiles!'

To repeat: if the particle is taken as guiding the reader to expect a re-presentation of a potential state of affairs, then the burden of proving whether or not this representation indicates purpose, potential result, or a recollection of an earlier prophetic statement is left to the judgement of the reader. The parallel passage in Matthew supports the view of representation and leads in to a further particle which we will consider below.

Matthew 13:13

> διὰ τοῦτο ἐν παραβολαῖς αὐτοῖς λαλῶ, ὅτι βλέποντες οὐ βλέπουσιν καὶ ἀκούοντες οὐκ ἀκούουσιν οὐδὲ συνίουσιν, καὶ ἀναπληροῦται αὐτοῖς ἡ προφητεία Ἠσαΐου ἡ λέγουσα . . .
>
> For this reason I speak to them in parables because/in that looking they do not see and listening they neither hear nor understand and the prophecy of Isaiah is being fulfilled which says . . .

The parallel passage to Mark 4:10-12 in Matthew 13:13 introduces a version of Isaiah 6:9-10 but uses participles together with verbs in the *indicative* mood, introduced by the particle ὅτι, thus presenting an actual situation rather than the potential one of the Marcan passage. As participles are famously underdetermined, they may be treated as concessive here: *although they see . . . although they hear*, which makes clear the opportunity presented to the crowd, but also their ignoring of it.

The Matthean passage explains that the reaction of the crowd fulfils the prophecy in Isaiah, but does not attribute Jesus' use of parables as a way of intentionally preventing some of his hearers from understanding his teaching. The way in which the passage in Isaiah is used in Matthew 13:15 clearly gives the hardness of heart of the people as the reason for the lack of understanding. The use of γάρ in this verse in Matthew and also in the Septuagint text of Isaiah 6:10 clarifies this: it gives supporting evidence for what has preceded it. The full text is subsequently quoted, but the purposive link between parables and preventing from hearing, seeing and turning is missing. The issue of verbal irony is also very relevant in the quotation from Isaiah as discussed in Chapter Four. At this point we should look again briefly at the particle ὅτι.

Ὅτι *as Introducing Re-presentation*

The particle ὅτι may be usefully regarded as operating in a manner parallel to that of ἵνα but giving procedural instructions to a reader or hearer to read the following text as describing *an actual state of affairs*, rather than the potential one ἵνα introduces. In simple terms, ὅτι introduces *a description of a situation*, whereas ἵνα introduces *a potential situation*: what the speaker or subject wants to see happening or thinks should be happening. Here the mood of the verbs in the corresponding clauses supports this analysis with the indicative indicating 'fact' – as presented by the speaker or subject – and the subjunctive indicating potentiality.

An example encountered in an earlier chapter illustrates this:

> Διὰ τί τοῦτο τὸ μύρον οὐκ ἐπράθη τριακοσίων δηναρίων καὶ ἐδόθη πτωχοῖς;
>
> εἶπεν δὲ τοῦτο **οὐχ ὅτι** περὶ τῶν πτωχῶν ἔμελεν αὐτῷ, **αλλ' ὅτι** κλέπτης ἦν καὶ τὸ γλωσσόκομον ἔχων τὰ βαλλόμενα ἐβάσταζεν.
>
> 'Why was this perfume not sold for three hundred denarii and given to the poor?'
>
> He said this not because he cared for the poor but because he was a thief and being responsible for the collecting bag he carried what was in it.[1]

1. John 12:5-6.

The two clauses introduced by ὅτι give two states of affairs, the first being negated, 'not that he cared for the poor', and the second giving a true state of affairs from the perspective of the writer: 'but because he was a thief'. In Chapter Two we considered this example from the perspective of the hearers. The speaker intended them to believe that by criticising the use of the perfume he was concerned for the poor, but the hearers – or at least one of them – believed otherwise. The author was employing the regular human ability to use a sophisticated understanding of what a speaker may be presenting as true but what the hearer suspects is untrue.

When something is presented as a 'state of affairs' it does not necessarily mean that it is true, but that the speaker is *presenting it as true*. The speaker may himself believe that the statement is true but be mistaken in that belief. Ὅτι was dealt with earlier when considering the way in which humans represent the words of others, but it is worth mentioning again here. It is clearly related to the use of ἵνα, but in this context it guides a hearer in interpreting what follows as an *actual*, rather than a potential, state of affairs.

Of course, this particle only points to the clause following it as indicating a re-presentation of a state of affairs. It may be a direct or indirect quotation, but this can only be decided pragmatically, by considering the pronouns used in the 'quotation'. As we noted before, 'resemblance', rather than identity, is all that we can claim. This has already been dealt with in Chapter Three, in which we considered re-presentation.

ὡς *Introducing a Re-presentation*

This is such a widely used particle in the NT that it may seem irrelevant to pick out one particular use only, but that use fits very well with the other particles being dealt with in this chapter. It introduces a representation, and is congruent with similar usage in the *Anabasis* of Xenophon. This particle regularly introduces a comparison or a metaphor, and this is its most common use in the NT, whether it leads on to a noun, adjective or clause. In addition, a positive may occur with a negative, particularly in the letters of Paul,[1] but also in Matthew 7:29 with a parallel passage in Mark 1:22:

1. 2 Corinthians 6:4-10

> ἦν γὰρ διδάσκων αὐτοὺς ὡς ἐξουσίαν ἔχων καὶ οὐχ ὡς οἱ γραμματεῖς αὐτῶν
>
> For he was teaching them as one who had authority and not as their scribes.

When this particle occurs with a participle it alerts the reader to interpret the following presentation as a potential situation, perhaps even one being presented as true by others but without being endorsed as such by the author. The following are examples of this use:

> Προσηνέγκατε μοι τὸν ἄνθρωπον τοῦτον ὡς ἀποστρέφοντα τὸν λαόν
>
> You brought this man to me as one stirring up the people.[1]
>
> τῶν δὲ ναυτῶν ζητούντων φυγεῖν ἐκ τοῦ πλοίου καὶ χαλασάντων τὴν σκάφην εἰς τὴν θάλασσαν προφάσει ὡς ἐκ πρῴρης ἀγκύρας μελλόντων ἐκτείνειν,
>
> but when the sailors, wanting to escape from the ship, lowered the dinghy into the sea on the pretext of being about to put out the anchors . . .
>
> ἀντιλεγόντων δὲ τῶν Ἰουδαίων ἠναγκάσθην ἐπικαλέσασθαι Καίσαρα οὐχ ὡς τοῦ ἔθνους μου ἔχων τι κατηγορεῖν
>
> But when the Jews spoke against me/it, I was compelled to appeal to Caesar, not as if I had anything to say against my nation.[2]

In these examples it can be seen that a presentation had been made which is being viewed as untrue by the speaker or writer – Pilate in the example from Luke, and Paul in the examples from Acts. The particle ὡς introduces such a presentation and together with the context alerts the reader to expect a statement that turned out to be untrue. In the Lucan example, the presentation that the rulers brought is articulated by Pilate as 'This man is stirring up the people'. Pilate is then portrayed as refuting this by stating that he has found no evidence of wrongdoing.

---

1. Luke 23:14.
2. Acts 27:30 and 28:19.

In the example from Acts 27:30, the sailors seem to have presented themselves as going to throw down the anchors, but the use of προφάσει together with ὡς indicates that while this may have been stated, it was not their actual intention.

In the second example from Acts, Paul is presented as claiming that his appeal to Caesar was necessitated not because of his complaint against his own people – as might well have been assumed by those Jews who visited him – but because the Jewish leaders who were present had spoken against his release, or against him personally when the Romans were minded to release him. Here the potential thought or assumption is introduced by ὡς, but prefaced by a negative.

It is important to remember that ὡς *by itself* indicates a re-presentation. That presentation may be thought by the speaker or author to be untrue, but only the context will reveal this. *It alerts the reader to proceed with caution.* The following examples from Xenophon are a good example of this. They alert the reader, and further information confirms that the author does not believe what is being presented.

Parallels from Xenophon's *Anabasis*

Xenophon uses this particle regularly to give the ostensive intention of a character but the reader understands that there is a hidden agenda. The following examples are given by Xenophon to show the covert way in which Cyrus gathered a large body of men to march against the Persian King. In each case Cyrus suggested plausibly and ostensively that he needed military support for a more local problem.[1]

ὡς ἐπιβουλεύοντος Τισσαφέρνους ταῖς πόλεσι.

As if Tissaphernes was plotting against the city states (MGS)
On the plea that Tissaphernes had designs against their cities. (Carleton Brownson)[2]

Here Cyrus is surreptitiously gathering troops but without giving the real reason for the draft.

In the next example he suggests to a friend, Proxenus, that the Pisidians are giving him trouble:

1. Ostension has been dealt with in Chapter Two.
2. *Anabasis* 1.1.6

> Πρόξενον δὲ τὸν Βοιώτιον ξένον ὄντα ἐκέλευσε λαβόντα ἄνδρας ὅτι πλείστους παραγενέσθαι, ὡς ἐς Πισίδας βουλόμενος στρατεύσθαι, ὡς πράγματα παρεχόντων τῶν Πισιδῶν τῇ ἑαυτοῦ χώρᾳ.
>
> He instructed a friend, Proxenus the Boeotian, to gather a large group of men and come to him, as he was planning a campaign against the Pisidians as (if) they were making trouble in his land.[1]

Both the clauses introduced by this particle represent a position which Cyrus was portraying as the reason for his request. They were plausible but in both cases it was not the real reason for the request. These reasons were ostensive: *I plan a campaign against the Pisidians . . . the Pisidians are making trouble*, but the reader is invited to use a strategy of *sophisticated understanding* in order to access the real reason for the request. The use of ὡς with a participle allows such a strategy. It gives *procedural instructions* to the reader. It is important to remember, however, that ὡς by itself indicates a re-presentation only. That presentation *may* be thought by the speaker or writer to be untrue, but only the context will reveal this. As stated above, it alerts the reader to proceed with caution. In the example from Acts 27:30 above, the use of προφάσις before this particle indicates that the ostensive reason for the sailors' moving to the side of the ship was to lower the anchors, but in fact they were planning to lower the dinghy and escape.

Καίπερ *as a Guiding Particle*[2]

In Koine as well as Classical Greek, participles have logical relations to the rest of the sentence in which they occur. The Greek participles are *underdetermined* in that they contain no marker to indicate such logical relationships.[3] The context will determine whether or not this relationship is one of time, cause, condition, or concession. Commentators and translators

1. Ibid, 1.1.11
2. A fuller version of the uses of this particle is found in M.G. Sim (2011) *Festschrift for Stephen Levinsohn* and the brief description here is used here with permission.
3. Robertson, A.T. (1934) *A Grammar of the Greek New Testament*. Nashville: Broadman Press, p. 1124. See also Sim (2004).

occasionally seem to employ intuitive guessing in determining such a logical relation, but the core principle of relevance should be applied. If there is a temporal relationship the addition of such adverbs as νῦν and ἄρτι may make this clear.[1]

The addition of this particle καίπερ, however, constrains the interpretation to one of concession. It is true that in terms of relevance there may be more than one possible logical relation for a participle. For example, there are scholarly debates about whether the participle ὑπάρχων in Philippians 2:6 indicates a concessive or a causal relation to the rest of the sentence.[2] The use of this particle καίπερ limits possible relationships to one of concession, as the following examples from the book of Hebrews shows.

> καίπερ ὤν υἱός, ἔμαθεν ἀφ' ὧν ἔπαθεν τὴν ὑπακοήν
>
> Although he was a son, he learned obedience through what he suffered.[3]

For many in the ancient world, the relationship between being a son and suffering in the pursuit of obedience was an accepted part of life. Indeed, the same author makes this point clearly in 12:5-11. The reader has to be guided away from this interpretation, however, although it would have been relevant, by the use of καίπερ and being directed to a concessive interpretation. If this small word had not been added, the most relevant relationship would have been one of cause, but the author has added καίπερ to block off that relationship and guide the reader to one of concession, showing that it is contrary to expectation.

That example is fairly straightforward but the author of Hebrews has two other examples of a participial clause accompanied by the particle καίπερ: 7:5 and 12:17, and in these it is not so easy to see the reason for the addition of this particle as a constraint.

> καὶ οἱ μὲν ἐκ τῶν υἱῶν Λευὶ τὴν ἱερατείαν λαμβάνοντες ἐντολὴν ἔχουσιν ἀποδεκατοῦν τὸν λαὸν κατὰ τὸν νόμον, τοῦτ' ἔστιν τοὺς ἀδελφοὺς αὐτῶν, καίπερ ἐξεληλυθότας ἐκ τῆς ὀσφύος Ἀβραάμ.

1. For example, 1 Thessalonians 3:6; 1 Peter 1:8 for ἄρτι and Luke 6:21; 2 Corinthians 13:2 for νῦν.
2. Wright, N.T. (1986) 'ἁρπαγμός and the Meaning of Philippians 2:5-11'. *JTS* 37, pp. 321-352.
3. Hebrews 5:8.

> The sons of Levi who received the priesthood have a command to take a tenth from the people according to the law, that is their brothers, although they have all come out from Abraham's body.

Without the particle καίπερ a concessive interpretation would not be the most relevant. It would seem to be merely extra information about the brothers of the Levites, reminding the reader about their common ancestry. The addition of the particle, however, highlights firstly the fact that it is *contrary to expectation* that members of the same family or clan group pay tithes to that group. Secondly, the expectation would be that the subservient would pay to a superior. The point that the author wishes to make is that even Abraham, from whom the whole ethnic group arose and whose descendants were instructed to collect tithes from their own brothers, gave tithes to Melchizedek, and so it could be said that even Levi paid tithes to this superior personage. Then, having established the superiority of Melchizedek, the author is able to show from Psalm 110:4 that Jesus belongs to a superior priesthood.

Hebrews 12:17

> ἴστε γὰρ ὅτι καὶ μετέπειτα θέλων κληρονομῆσαι τὴν εὐλογίαν ἀπεδοκιμάσθη, μετανοίας γὰρ τόπον οὐχ εὗρεν καίπερ μετὰ δακρύων ἐκζητήσας αὐτήν.
>
> For you know that afterwards when he wanted to inherit the blessing he was disqualified, for he did not find a place of turning back/change of mind, although he looked for it with tears.

Again there is a statement here that is contrary to expectation: one who 'looks for repentance/turning back' should surely find it, particularly if this was a serious endeavour. The lesson being impressed on the readers, however, is that there will be no possibility of turning back to revisit and alter an event that has already taken place. The Greek might be translated as 'place of changing' with reference to changing Isaac's blessing of Jacob, but such changing could no longer be possible. This also accords with the account of Esau's grief in Genesis 27:34-38. There may be forgiveness, but the original act cannot be wiped out. In this example also, the principle of relevance is involved in determining the 'meaning' of the underdetermined μετανοία as 'change of mind', or, as noted above, 'place of changing', rather than the concept of 'repentance' which is selected for this word in other parts of the New Testament. N.T. Wright draws out the implicatures in this utterance by the following translation:

> There was no way he could change either his mind or Isaac's, even though he wept bitterly in trying to do so.

It was not only his own changing that was the issue, but his father Isaac's giving of the blessing for the first born to Jacob.[1]

Εὐθύς *as a Guiding Adverb*

Another particle – or rather adverb – is used to direct the reader to process the following event as occurring very soon after the previous one, but the traditional translation of 'immediately' in English does not fit well on many occasions. This is εὐθύς, a Marcan favourite. Of the fifty-four occurrences of this adverb in the NT, forty-two are in Mark's Gospel. The idea of the adverb seems to be *constraining the temporal sequence of the following event to show its consecutive nature.* To translate this using the English 'immediately' sounds pedantic and quite unnatural in many cases. To avoid the unnaturalness, some translations omit the word altogether, but then the signal of one event following close on another is lost or at least opaque. The following examples make this clear:

> καὶ εὐθὺς ἦν ἐν τῷ συναγωγῇ αὐτῶν ἄνθρωπος ἐν πνεύματι ἀκαθάρτῳ καὶ ἀνέκραξεν
>
> and then in their synagogue there was a man with an unclean spirit and he cried out . . .[2]

The context here shows that Jesus was already in the synagogue and had been teaching there. The addition of this adverb may suggest that the man interrupted the teaching, or at least that the disturbance occurred very soon afterwards. There are eleven occurrences of this adverb in the first chapter of Mark, one quarter

1. Wright, T. (2011) *New Testament for Everyone*. London: SPCK.
2. Mark 1:23.

of all the examples. The way in which this article is translated in modern versions is very interesting: 'as he was coming out'; 'at once' twice; 'without delay'; 'when the Sabbath came'; 'just then'; 'quickly'; 'as soon as'; omit; 'immediately'; 'at once'.[1] Such translations are operating pragmatically in that they are giving in English what they see to be the function of the Greek adverb. It isn't possible to give a single translation for this, but only to recognise that it is giving procedural instructions to the reader to expect a follow-on, without a break from the previous action and, in some cases, the context even suggests simultaneity.

Γάρ *as Supporting Previous Information or Comments*

I plan to deal with this particle very briefly since it was examined several years ago by the late Dr Regina Blass and is now the subject of a doctoral thesis by Sarah Casson.[2] The particle is ubiquitous in certain portions of the NT, particularly in the Letter to the Romans, and this frequency has led many translators to ignore it completely in English. N.T. Wright, however, in the preface to his *New Testament for Everyone* points out the inappropriateness of a bland translation of 'for' or 'because'.[3] He claims that Paul uses this particle 'to connect his sentences', and this is true, but I would like to take this further and suggest that γάρ does not only connect sentences, but gives the reader instructions in processing the utterance γάρ introduces.[4]

γάρ supports statements or arguments that have gone before, but not necessarily in the immediately preceding sentence. One example that shows the complex nature of such support occurs in all three Synoptic Gospels: Matthew 19:22; Mark 10:22 and Luke 18:23.

> ὁ δὲ ἀκούσας ταῦτα περίλυπος ἐγενήθη· ἦν γὰρ πλούσιος σφόδρα.
>
> But when he heard this he was sad, for he was very wealthy.[5]

---

1. These phrases account for the occurrences of εὐθύς in Mark 1 in NIV.
2. Sarah Casson is studying at King's College, London, and the thesis should be completed by 2017.
3. Wright (2011) p. xiv-xv.
4. Ibid, p. xiv.
5. Luke 18:23.

The point here is not that he was sad because of his wealth, but because of the link between following Jesus and the need to give away this wealth to the needy. The particle supports the reason for his grief: not only his wealth but his attachment to it. Recognising this then makes it easier to process the following comment made by Jesus:

> How hard it is for those who have many possessions to enter the kingdom of God.[1]

It is not the possession of wealth that causes the problem but an attachment to such possessions. In the Lucan version given above, the phrase 'when Jesus saw him looking sad' is added to link the young man's reaction and the subsequent comment about the difficulty of having wealth. Matthew and Mark mention his 'going away sad' before the clause with γὰρ, which reinforces the link between attachment to wealth and the difficulty of following Jesus.

A further unexpected use of this particle occurs in the Acts of the Apostles 8:39, in the conclusion of the account of the Ethiopian official whom Philip met:

> ὅτε δὲ ἀνέβησαν ἐκ τοῦ ὕδατος, πνεῦμα κυρίου ἥρπασεν τὸν Φίλιππον καὶ οὐκ εἶδεν αὐτὸν οὐκέτι ὁ εὐνοῦχος, ἐπορεύετο γὰρ τὴν ὁδὸν αὐτοῦ χαίρων.
>
> When they came up out of the water the Spirit of the Lord seized Philip and the eunuch no longer saw him, for he went on his journey rejoicing.

The NIV translates the γὰρ in this verse as 'but', which might seem more logical, but apart from the fact that this particle is not contrastive, such a translation does not bring out the force of the outcome that the author was presenting: the Ethiopian no longer needed Philip and went away in a transformed state of mind. The particle gives evidence for this change which the previous narrative has led up to. F.F. Bruce comments on the difference between this outcome and that of the rich young ruler that we have noted above.[2] Haenchen, noting the parallel

1. Luke 18:24.
2. Bruce, F.F. (1976, 3rd edition) *The Acts of the Apostles*, Leicester: IVP, p. 195.

between the Spirit taking Philip and the taking of Elijah in 2 Kings 2:12, points out that the sons of the prophets spent three days looking for Elijah while the Ethiopian 'continues joyfully on his way'.[1]

Barrett alone deals with the issue of γάρ:

> γὰρ is at first surprising but is explained by an ellipse. The sense is: The eunuch saw no more of Philip, for he, unlike Philip, was not supernaturally removed but simply continued his journey.[2]

I do not see the need for an 'ellipse', but I do appreciate his understanding of the appropriate use of this particle. There are over 1,000 occurrences of γάρ in the NT, and these require a dedicated study, but these few examples have been presented to support the idea of this particle as giving instructions to the reader to process the following sentence as supporting evidence for what has gone before. A bland translation of 'for' or 'because' does not always bring out the relevance of this support, but understanding the function of the particle is a better guide to successful exegesis. By 'successful', I mean communicatively relevant!

Οὖν *as Indicating Relevance*

This particle is very common in the New Testament and in particular in John, but this use is not aberrant. What is unusual, however, is the distribution of its use in John, with a total of 207 out of 491 examples in the NT, but no examples whatsoever in chapters 14, 15 and 17.

I suggest that the particle has been too narrowly categorised, with scholars[3] (and lexicons) giving a descriptive account of its use as: resumptive, showing close connection, beginning of new unit, inferential, contrastive, development marker etc.[4] I do not disagree with this analysis, disparate as it is, but hope to show that such relationships are pragmatically determined and are not an intrinsic

1. Haenchen, E. (1971) *The Acts of the Apostles.* Oxford: Blackwell, p. 313.
2. Barrett, C.K. (1994) *Acts* Vol. 1. Edinburgh: T. & T. Clark, p. 434.
3. A.T. Robertson is, as usual, a glorious exception and his wise words are discussed below!
4. Abbott (1906), Buth (1992), Levinsohn (2000), Robertson (1934).

feature of the particle. I will suggest a more explanatory, less purely descriptive, account of its use. Descriptive accounts relate to the context in which the particle occurs, but do not show its function.

Another way in which scholars have accounted for the quite different usage by the writer of the fourth Gospel is by citing his unique 'style'. Using this term, however, we sidestep the communicative issue. When a speaker/writer uses particular words which we may commonly refer to as his 'style', he is making a choice, although not always a conscious one, to influence his hearer/reader and to cause her to draw inferences from such use.[1] We can see this even in the modern colloquial use of short phrases such as 'you know' and 'know what I mean' which hope to elicit a positive response from the hearer, indicating that the speaker is making himself relevant.

Use of This Particle in John's Gospel

As stated earlier, we find around two hundred (some examples in textual variants) instances of οὖν in the Gospel of John, but none at all in the Johannine epistles. The use is not evenly distributed, but it is certainly more common in narrative portions of this Gospel and in dialogue within those narrative portions. The heavy use in some chapters is partly accounted for by its use in speech margins, for example in 8:12-30 and 11:12-16. Before attempting to give an analysis which claims explanatory adequacy rather than merely descriptive adequacy I want to look at several passages from the Gospel of John so that we can examine the way in which the particle is used. I have selected 4:1-11 and 4:5-53 and chapter 18.

Although commentators have noted the 'resumptive' force of οὖν, they do not seem to have acknowledged the verbal correspondence which very frequently accompanies this particle. Looking first at chapter 4:1-11, we can note the repetition of vocabulary:

> 4:1 ὡς οὖν ἔγνων ὁ Ἰησοῦς ὅτι ἤκουσαν οἱ Φαρισαῖοι ὅτι Ἰησοῦς πλείονας μαθητὰς ποιεῖ καὶ βαπτίζει ἢ Ἰωάννης
>
> So when Jesus knew that the Pharisees had heard that Jesus was making and baptising more disciples than John . . .

1. As in other chapters I am using the male personal pronoun to refer to the speaker or writer, and the female pronoun to refer to the hearer or reader.

This takes the reader back to 3:22-23 and 3:25 after a discussion covering the position of John and Jesus with 'John' 'baptising' and 'disciples' being common terms.

4:5 ἔρχεται οὖν εἰς πόλιν τῆς Σαμαρείας.

So he comes to a town of Samaria . . .

4:6 ἦν δὲ ἐκεῖ πηγὴ τοῦ Ἰακώβ. ὁ οὖν Ἰησοῦς κεκοπιακὼς ἐκ τῆς ὁδοιπορίας ἐκαθέζετο οὕτως ἐπὶ τῇ πηγῇ.

Jacob's well was there. So Jesus, exhausted from travelling, was sitting down there at the well.

The verb in verse 5 picks up the 'coming' of the previous verse as well as 'Samaria'. The second sentence of verse 6 picks up 'well' from the first sentence, and the motif of travelling. Verse 8 gives support or explanation for Jesus requesting a drink, not from his disciples, but from a woman who happens to come to that well.

4:9 λέγει οὖν αὐτῷ ἡ γυνὴ ἡ Σαμαρῖτις . . .

Then the Samaritan woman says to him . . .

This mirrors the vocabulary of 7, and connects with both the woman and Jesus after the explanatory verse 8. Verse 10 is the response of Jesus, and then in verse 11 the particle features again to bring some of the content of verse 10 into discussion:

4:11 λέγει αὐτῷ [ἡ γυνή]· κύριε, οὔτε ἄντλημα ἔχεις καὶ τὸ φρέαρ ἐστὶν βαθύ· πόθεν οὖν τὸ ὕδωρ τὸ ζῶν;

The woman says to him, 'Sir, you do not have a receptacle and the well is deep. So from where do you have the living water?'

The 'living water' is a quote from the words of Jesus' response in verse 10 but note in passing that the relevance of the woman's response is derived from pragmatic inference: water comes from a well, but the only way of getting it out is via some kind of container.[1] The particle appears again in verse 28:

4:28 ἀφῆκεν οὖν τὴν ὑδρίαν αὐτῆς ἡ γυνὴ καὶ ἀπῆλθεν εἰς τὴν πόλιν

Then the woman left her water pot and went back to the town . . .

1. RT describes this type of inference as being a 'bridging assumption'.

This brings 'the woman' back into the picture after verse 27 discusses the return of the disciples with food. The particle does not appear from 12-27, when there is a discussion about worship and the varying practice of Jews and Samaritans with very little in the way of overt marking by any 'discourse' particles. Pragmatic inferencing makes the connection.

4:45 ὅτε οὖν ἦλθεν εἰς τὴν Γαλιλαίαν, ἐδέξαντο αὐτὸν οἱ Γαλιλαῖοι πάντα ἑωρακότες ὅσα ἐποίησεν ἐν Ἱεροσολύμοις

So when he came to Galilee the Galileans received him having seen what he did in Jerusalem . . .

4:46 ἦλθεν οὖν πάλιν εἰς τὴν Κανὰ τῆς Γαλιλαίας, ὅπου ἐποίησεν τὸ ὕδωρ οἶνον.

So he came again to Cana in Galilee where he made the water wine.

This verse not only recaps the vocabulary of the previous verse about the move to Galilee, but recalls the first 'sign' which gives the background to the response of Jesus in verse 48, again introduced by οὖν:

4:48 εἶπεν οὖν ὁ Ἰησοῦς πρὸς αὐτόν· ἐὰν μὴ σημεῖα καὶ τέρατα ἴδητε, οὐ μὴ πιστεύσητε.

Then Jesus said to him 'If you don't see signs and wonders you won't believe.'

4:50-53 λέγει αὐτῷ ὁ Ἰησοῦς· πορεύου, ὁ υἱός σου ζῇ. ἐπίστευσεν ὁ ἄνθρωπος τῷ λόγῳ ὃν εἶπεν αὐτῷ ὁ Ἰησοῦς καὶ ἐπορεύετο.

ἤδη δὲ αὐτοῦ καταβαίνοντος οἱ δοῦλοι αὐτοῦ ὑπήντησαν αὐτῷ λέγοντες ὅτι ὁ παῖς ζῇ.

ἐπύθετο οὖν τὴν ὥραν παρ' αὐτῶν ἐν ᾗ κομψότερον ἔσχεν· εἶπαν οὖν αὐτῷ ὅτι ἐχθὲς ὥραν ἑβδόμην ἀφῆκεν αὐτὸν ὁ πυρετός.

ἔγνω οὖν ὁ πατὴρ ὅτι [ἐν] ἐκείνῃ τῇ ὥρᾳ ἐν ᾗ εἶπεν αὐτῷ ὁ Ἰησοῦς· ὁ υἱός σου ζῇ, καὶ ἐπίστευσεν αὐτὸς καὶ ἡ οἰκία αὐτοῦ ὅλη.

Jesus said to him, 'Go, your son lives'. The man believed the word which Jesus spoke to him and went away.

> As he was travelling down his slaves met him saying 'The child lives'.
>
> Then he inquired from them the time at which he became better. So they told him it was yesterday at the seventh hour that the fever left him. Then the father knew that at that hour Jesus had said to him 'Your son lives' and he himself believed and his whole household.

The particle here picks up the information from verse 50 that the man believed and went away. While he was still on his way, he was greeted by his servants with good news. The phrase 'your son lives' occurs three times (once with a change of noun). In addition, the verbs 'going' and 'believing' are repeated both in the speech of Jesus and in the narrative of the man's arriving home. The occurrence of οὖν in verse 48 prefaces a seemingly harsh response to the father's desperate appeal, which is then followed by a more positive commitment.

In 18:3-19, οὖν appears in almost every verse with repetition of vocabulary being a feature in many of these verses (3, 6, 7, 8, 12, 16 and 17). This is not the main function of this particle, but it frequently occurs with vocabulary that has been part of earlier text. This is not limited to John, or even the NT, but there are examples from Xenophon and Epictetus that make such repetition seem a logical concomitant of a particle which is described as 'resumptive'.[1] In other words, it is not only the particle that is 'resumptive', but there are verbal correlations also that aid this interpretation and to which the particle may point.

Xenophon's Use of Οὖν

Although this author doesn't use this particle as frequently as John, his use is comparable with that of the NT, as the following chart taken from Jannaris' *Historical Greek Grammar* shows:

	Thuc.	Xen.1-3	prop.	Polyb.	NT to Col	NT whole
οὖν	236	67	400	324	437	491

In the first three books of his *Anabasis*, Xenophon uses this particle sixty-seven times as well as using οὐκοῦν when expecting a positive answer to a question. The proportionate use (400)

1. Xenophon, *Anabasis,* 2.1.12, 2.1.17. Epictetus, *Discourses,* 1.4.16,17; 1.7.6,7.

which Jannaris gives shows that, in the same amount of text, the NT is not unusual in its use. I give one example only to show that our understanding of the inferences we are expected to draw comes from the context, and not from the semantic content of the particle itself. This sentence comes in 1.9.1 in the middle of a narrative which describes the death of Cyrus followed by a paean to his noble character:

> Κῦρος μὲν οὖν οὕτως ἐτελεύτησεν, ἀνὴρ ὢν Περσῶν τῶν μετὰ Κῦρον τὸν ἀρχαῖον γενομένων
> βασιλικώτατος τε καὶ ἄρχειν ἀξιώτατος . . .
>
> So Cyrus died like this, being a most kingly man and most worthy to rule of all the Persians after Cyrus the Elder . . .

The actual account of the death of Cyrus began three sentences earlier, but was immediately followed by a description of his companions who died with him. The particle then, in structuralist terms, is resumptive, picking up the death of Cyrus and continuing to give honour to the dead man. I suggest, however, that it gives the reader reassurance of the relevance of the communication before giving further information about Cyrus himself.

Epictetus' Use of Οὖν

In previous chapters I have used examples from the *Discourses* of Epictetus, which were recorded by Arrian. As noted in Chapter One, Epictetus was a contemporary of Paul and many features of his language are reflected in the letters of that apostle. The count for his use of this particle in these writings is 850 (in 80,000 words), but I counted 230 instances in the first book alone.[1] This fact should make necessary a rethink of the common belief that John's use of οὖν is aberrant. Of course, the *Discourses* are not narrative, but diatribe. It is still clear, however, that this particle could have been widely used in the first century CE and, from Xenophon, we can see that even earlier writers of narrative were not far behind the usage of the NT.

1. The total number of words in the Greek New Testament is said to be 137,490, which means that the figures for the occurrences of this particle in Epictetus are much higher than in either the NT or John's Gospel!

A Fresh Look at Οὖν

As with the other particles, we do not interpret utterances by deciphering a code, but by a process of inferencing which may use semantic concepts but which then draws out implications from contextual and encyclopaedic information. Putting it simply, it is not the 'meaning' of individual words that give understanding of utterances, but the whole background of shared knowledge between speaker and hearer as well as the surrounding narrative.

Blakemore claims that 'the expressions which have been labelled as discourse markers must be analysed in terms of their input to those (cognitive) processes'.[1] My question is: what did a writer want his reader to infer from the use of οὖν? Alternatively: in what way does the particle help the reader to derive the most relevant reading of the text? The procedural instruction that the particle οὖν gives is: 'this is still relevant'! In other words it encourages the reader to proceed with the text in the belief that the new information is pertinent and directly related to what has gone before. This is particularly necessary if there has been a small digression, as frequently (but not always) happens before the introduction of οὖν.

As I have examined this particle in NT and pagan Greek, I have come to see that it is the supreme indicator of relevance for a reader. Consider the frequent use in question after some dialogue or argument: τί οὖν what then?/so what?[2] It encourages a reader to continue. To quote A.T. Robertson:

> It just carries along the narrative with no necessary thought of cause or result.[3]

What we can add to this are the logical constraints that this particle does *not* provide: it does not support what has gone before, as γάρ does, in the sense of giving a reason or cause, and it does not contradict what has gone before. Moulton and Geden give one 'meaning' as 'adversative', but it is the context

1. Blakemore, D. (2002) *Relevance and Linguistic Meaning*. Cambridge: CUP, p. 5.
2. John 1:21, 25; 6:30; Romans 3:1, 9; 4:1; 6:1 among many others, as well as Epictetus 1.1.13, 17, 21, 27, etc.
3. Robertson (1934) p. 1191.

that leads them to make this analysis and it is only one potential analysis, with the 'contrast' being mainly in the mind of the interpreter![1]

I would extend that to claim that οὖν encourages the reader to keep on processing by assuring her of the relevance of the new material. We do not first need to identify consciously either the topic or the resumptive nature of this new material. After all, we only know it is resumptive because there is an intervening piece of information. It is not part of the semantic content of the particle. Blakemore again:

> If a hearer identifies a coherence relation, then it is as a result of successful comprehension rather than a prerequisite for it.[2]

Conclusion

This chapter is a plea for a move to an understanding of particles in terms of how we communicate rather than the identification of a taxonomy of potential relations in discourse. It invites us to examine the way in which biblical text achieves relevance both for the original readers and for those of us who follow them. Many particles in Greek are not susceptible to a one word translation. They are *underdetermined*, to use the expression introduced in earlier chapters. They give procedural instructions to the reader to read or interpret what follows in a particular way. Some of these are almost self-evident – the basic meaning of the adjective εὐθύς is 'straight' from which the old KJV translated 'straightway' and the general idea of immediacy follows. The particle ἵνα on the other hand cannot be treated to a 'one size fits all', but rather as a marker of a re-presentation of a desirable or necessary state of affairs.

1. Several examples are given as alternatives by Moulton and Geden (John 8:5, Acts 17:30; 1 Corinthians 11:20; 15:11), which show the openness of this particle's instructions. Moulton and Geden (1897) *Concordance to the Greek New Testament.* Edited by I. Howard Marshall. Edinburgh: T. & T. Clark, 2002, pp. 798-802.
2. Blakemore (2002) p. 169.

I append here a brief summary of my suggestions for these particles:

- ἵνα introduces a potential state of affairs;
- ὅτι by contrast introduces an actual state of affairs, from the perspective of the speaker;
- ὡς alerts the reader to expect a re-presentation that may not in fact be a true state of affairs;
- καίπερ constrains the logical relations possible with participles;
- γάρ supports previous material while
- οὖν asserts the relevance of new material.

Chapter 6
Conditional Sentences

The logical relationship found between clauses in conditional sentences in the NT has often raised difficulties for readers, leading to serious heart-searching over such statements as 'If your eye offends you pluck it out' for those with sensitive consciences! Daniel Wallace, in introducing a chapter on this topic claims that:

> On any Sunday misinformation about conditional clauses is communicated from pulpit to pew. Whole theological systems and life styles are sometimes built on such misunderstandings.[1]

I don't share his anxiety about this, but it is certainly true that conditional clauses may cause unease and be used to support a thoroughly unsound argument. It is also important to remember that a grammatical form may be deceptive. Not all conditional sentences begin with 'if', but commands and (in Koine Greek) participles may also occupy the slot in which we might have expected to see an 'if' clause:

> Do that again and you will lose your job!

This example shows the way in which a command form may be used without any expectation that the hearer will obey – in fact, it's a threat, rather than a command! In pragmatic terms, this utterance functions as a conditional sentence indicating to a hearer that certain behaviour will result in dismissal.

Conditional clauses may be used with less than literal import, instead making a serious point about the consequences of an action, as we can see from the example cited above from Mark

1. Wallace, D. (1996, 4th revised edition) *Greek Grammar Beyond the Basics*. GR, Michigan: Zondervan. p. 681.

9:47. The two clauses taken together impress the hearer with the seriousness of allowing physical desires to take control. The context in Mark is that of offence to 'one of these little ones', a phrase often taken to refer to new or vulnerable believers. Hindering or offending such vulnerable ones is presented as a crime deserving of heavy punishment, and the one susceptible to such temptation should take drastic personal action to avoid offending. The context in which this verse is placed in Matthew's Gospel is Jesus' receiving a child and presenting him as a model to which the disciples should aspire in terms of humble behaviour, but the verses about the danger of offending 'one of these little ones who believe in me' follow on immediately. A picture of the need for severe action is presented allegorically in physical terms: if you are going to cause offence by where you go, what you do or what you look at, then you should avoid all such behaviour. In our modern world, so much offence has been caused to children and vulnerable 'little ones' that this picture is far from being too strong.

From a grammatical perspective, however, two different 'types' of condition are used. Matthew has a protasis introduced by εἰ with present tense verb form and a command for the apodosis. Mark, on the other hand, has ἐὰν with a verb in the subjunctive mood and again a command in the apodosis. This is a good example of the issue we'll address below: context tells us how to interpret a condition in terms of reality or unreality, and not the syntactic form.

Background in Koine

The usual definition of a conditional sentence is one that has a protasis; that is, an 'if' clause, followed by an apodosis giving the result (or a 'then' clause). Work on conditional sentences in Koine Greek has focused largely on syntax in identifying 'types' of condition, using either temporal forms or moods to elucidate the relationship between protasis and apodosis. Such syntactic clues have also been customarily used to identify 'real' or 'unreal' conditions, and even to claim that certain clauses are 'true' or 'untrue' on the basis of grammar. By contrast, RT approaches to conditionals in English (Noh 2000) have taken account of the role of meta-representation in the construction of the protasis in particular, giving a more satisfactory account of sentences that contain widely differing types of 'if' clauses.[1] I propose to demonstrate the relevance for exegesis of an approach which links syntax with inferences by drawing out the re-presentation of an utterance which is implicit in conditionals in Koine. Stanley Porter has suggested that a more flexible approach to such clauses is needed and I hope to provide this by drawing examples from the NT and pagan Greek.[2]

At the outset I must make clear that, in both English and Koine, whether or not a clause contains a statement that is true or factual is determined by the context and *not* by the form of the condition. Conditional sentences are concerned with a relation between two clauses and *not* with fact or non-fact. It is only the context that is able to indicate what is fact and what is not. The statement of a situation is all the syntax can give us. Of course, we can view a conditional sentence as a speaker's presentation of a statement *as if* it is a fact but that does not alter the need for a contextual identification. Daniel Wallace makes the focus of his chapter structural and semantic approaches only. Wallace gives himself away in his comment that 'the pragmatic approach is too far removed from form for us to get an easy handle on it; that is, it more properly belongs to discourse analysis than to syntax'.[3] This is not about 'getting an easy handle on it', but understanding how language works. It is more relevant that we see the communicative effect that a speaker hopes to achieve rather than pin down the condition to a particular 'type'.

A Brief Outline of Traditional Grammatical Analysis of Conditional Sentences

Before going on to discuss the RT approach to this topic, it will be useful to clear the ground by looking at the way conditional sentences are presented in standard grammars of Koine Greek. A.T. Robertson, as ever, is the voice of reason, coming from his deep knowledge of Classical and Koine Greek:

1. Meta-representation or re-presentation is dealt with in Chapter Three.
2. Porter, S. (1992) *Idioms of the Greek New Testament*. Sheffield: Sheffield Academic Press, pp. 254ff.
3. Wallace (1996) p. 681.

> We must distinguish always therefore between the fact and the statement of the fact. The conditional sentence deals only with the statement.
>
> The Greek is perspicuous if one will only give it a chance to speak for itself.[1]

Robertson deserves much more serious consideration than he has hitherto received. He outlines what subsequently came to be the position of the traditional Greek grammars such as Blass and Debrunner.[2] They describe Robertson's scheme as 'lucid', and so I have repeated below his suggested classes of condition in order to give a starting point. I am outlining these 'types' not because they will help us to determine the communicative purpose of the speaker, but in order to set out the problems that face exegetes when confronted with conditional sentences, and as a starting point from which to move ahead in a more perspicacious manner. These 'types' have been posited in order to guide exegetes through different syntactic forms, but the aim of defining whether or not an utterance is 'real' or 'unreal' cannot be decided by grammar alone.

There are usually four types of clauses set out, the basis for these being syntactic:

1. This class *assumes that the condition is real* and that the conclusion will follow from it. The indicative is the mood used.
2. This class deals with a protasis which is assumed to be *contrary to fact*. It may be true, but it is treated as untrue. Again, the indicative is the mood used but the tense is usually past and there may be ἂν or ἐὰν in the apodosis.
3. The protasis here indicates *potentiality rather than actuality*, but the apodosis looks for a positive outcome. ἐὰν with a verb in subjunctive mood is used in the protasis.
4. Sometimes this almost approximates to an indirect question. The optative mood is used in the protasis.

---

1. Robertson (1934) pp. 1006-7.
2. Blass, F., Debrunner, A., and Funk, R.W. (1961) *A Greek Grammar of the New Testament and Other Early Christian Literature*. Chicago: Chicago University Press, sect. 371-3.

Blass and Debrunner comment:

> The lack of any generally accepted terminology makes easy reference difficult. The classical grammars are also hopelessly at variance.[1]

These types are usually labelled as 'determined'(1) and (2) or 'undetermined' (3): 'determination' in the context of conditional clauses refers to an outcome when an 'if' clause is found to be true. As stated above, only the context can determine whether or not this clause is true, but in traditional grammars scholars have been struggling to link grammatical forms to 'outcomes'. Either pragmatic inferences are brought in to decide on the truth or otherwise of such clauses, *or* the types are decided from the context and grammatical forms identified in order to give 'evidence' for the differences. The fact of these decisions being inferences are not customarily acknowledged. This is the reason for my attempt to outline a more useful way of reading these sentences.

Charting a New Course

It is of course the case that many of these 'classes' or 'types' mentioned in the previous section are mixed in the NT, and in Modern Greek they have reduced the conditional particle to άν with the indicative and the apodoses can be very varied. Although Holton, Mackridge, and Philippaki-Warburton in their *Grammar of Modern Greek* talk of 'factual' and 'counterfactual' conditions, these are determined inevitably by the context and *not* by syntax. I propose we move away from these categories because, although they are defined on the basis of syntax alone, the context is then brought in to support a syntactic analysis, as noted above. In real life, we decide on the actuality or potentiality of a conditional sentence *on pragmatic terms alone.* This is particularly true in modern English, where the subjunctive that used to give a clue to an 'unreal' condition has more or less disappeared from the speech of speakers under the age of 40 years.[2]

1. Blass and Debrunner (1961) p. 189, sect. 371. They number the classes differently based on classical usage, but since they state that their class 2 'is barely represented in the NT' and class 5 does not appear at all, I have adopted Robertson's numbering.
2. Note the older speech forms of English 'If I were . . . I would . . .' which alerted a hearer to the possible non-factual nature of the

The main issue in a conditional sentence is the relationship between the two clauses. *If p, then q.* The assertion made in the protasis is being treated as true, even if in fact it is false. **I am suggesting that the protasis is a re-presentation of something which is known, has been said, or has been inferred.** We are then considering *not* whether or not a protasis is true or false, real or unreal, but how the speaker or writer is using it to carry on his argument *in continuity with* what has gone before. We can surmise the 'truth' or otherwise of the assertion, but in terms of what the writer is communicating, dealing with the protasis as re-presentation is much more useful in exegetical terms.

Examples of Re-presentation

I present below a straightforward example of the conditional clause as re-presentation. This sets out a non-controversial passage first, before we move onto more complicated examples. Without attempting to denigrate earlier scholars or to deny the different syntactic features which may appear in conditional clauses, I am suggesting that a new approach may be more helpful in determining the *communicative* purpose in the use of a conditional form. Syntactic features give clues, but they must be enriched by the drawing of inferences, as we have been discussing all through this book, in order to arrive at the true nature of the conditional sentence. We can suspect that the use of a past tense in a conditional sentence in Koine gives an indication of 'unreality', or even that the speaker's belief is that the protasis is false, but this is not always borne out by evidence. It is to context, background knowledge, and encyclopaedic information that we look for actual identification of reality or unreality.

1 Corinthians 15:12-19

The context here is Paul's rebuttal of an assertion: 'there is no resurrection of the dead', ἀνάστασις νεκρῶν οὐκ ἔστιν. The section follows one in which examples of Christ appearing to various people have been described, with many of these people being well-known to the Corinthians, such as Cephas, the 'twelve', James, and Paul himself. The content of the tradition

---

protasis. Agatha Christie used such a construction to alert a murderer to the fact that he had been seen in *Death on the Nile*.

that had been passed on to Paul (15:3-4) was also the content of the preaching: Christ was raised on the third day, according to the Scriptures. This is the background that leads on to the concatenation of conditional clauses from verse 12 to verse 19.

> 12. εἰ δὲ Χριστὸς κηρύσσεται ὅτι ἐκ νεκρῶν ἐγήγερται, πῶς λέγουσιν ἐν ὑμῖν τινες ὅτι ἀνάστασις νεκρῶν οὐκ ἔστιν;
>
> If Christ is preached that he has been risen from the dead, how do some people say that there is no resurrection of the dead?

Here the protasis clearly represents what constituted the apostolic preaching as noted in verses 4-9 of this chapter as being handed down by tradition. The apodosis in this verse then introduces the position which Paul is anxious to refute. This is not presented as preaching but 'saying', and suggests a movement on the part of some of the members of the churches in Corinth to deny the resurrection of believers, although they might accept the resurrection of Christ. In the subsequent verses, Paul moves logically from one step to another, but always uses the protasis to lay out the assertion which he hopes to refute. He then uses the apodosis to take the argument forward.

> 13. εἰ δὲ ἀνάστασις νεκρῶν οὐκ ἔστιν, οὐδὲ Χριστὸς ἐγήγερται.
>
> But if there is no resurrection of the dead, not even Christ has been raised.

Again the protasis picks up the apodosis of the previous condition: *there is no resurrection of the dead*, and gives the logical conclusion in good syllogistic fashion. No one rises from the dead; Christ was dead, therefore he has not risen.

> 14. εἰ δὲ Χριστὸς οὐκ ἐγήγερται, κενὸν ἄρα [καὶ] τὸ κήρυγμα ἡμῶν, κενὴ καὶ ἡ πίστις ὑμῶν.
>
> But if Christ has not been raised, then our preaching is empty and your faith is in vain.

The protasis is again taking up the apodosis of the previous sentence and asserting in the new apodosis that the content of the preaching is empty, as is their belief/faith *if* that claim in the protasis is true. In fact, he runs on to two assertions that are potential and conditional.

> 15. εὑρισκόμεθα δὲ καὶ ψευδομάρτυρες τοῦ θεοῦ, ὅτι ἐμαρτυρήσαμεν κατὰ τοῦ θεοῦ ὅτι ἤγειρεν τὸν Χριστόν, ὃν οὐκ ἤγειρεν εἴπερ ἄρα νεκροὶ οὐκ ἐγείρονται.
>
> But we are found also to be false witnesses of/falsely representing God, because/in that we witness of God that he raised the Christ, whom he did not raise if/then the dead are not raised.

Here the protasis comes at the end of the sentence but the initial clause is a further conclusion from the previous protasis: *Christ has not been raised.* A further conclusion is that *We are also found to be false witnesses of God because we have given evidence that he has raised the Christ whom he has not raised* ***if there is no resurrection of the dead.***

This latter argument is reinforced in the next verse:

> 16. εἰ γὰρ νεκροὶ οὐκ ἐγείρονται, οὐδὲ Χριστὸς ἐγήγερται.
>
> For if the dead are not raised, not even Christ has been raised.

This makes clear what was assumed in the previous verse and lays out Paul's position that the resurrection of the dead is inseparably linked with God's raising of Christ and this position is made even more clearly in 17-19.

> 17-18. εἰ δὲ Χριστὸς οὐκ ἐγήγερται, ματαία ἡ πίστις ὑμῶν, ἔτι ἐστε ἐν ταῖς ἁμαρτίαις ὑμῶν, ἄρα καὶ οἱ κοιμηθέντες ἐν Χριστῷ ἀπώλοντο.
>
> But if Christ has not been raised, your faith is futile and you are still in your sins and then those who have died in Christ have perished.

Again, the protasis is a representation of the apodosis of verse 16 as well as verse 15 and the protasis of verse 14. The apodosis presents a conclusion that the hearers would be reluctant to accept: their faith is in vain, they are still in their sins, and those who have died are 'lost'. The next verse takes this further by presenting a presupposition as the protasis:

19. εἰ ἐν τῇ ζωῇ ταύτῃ ἐν Χριστῷ ἠλπικότες ἐσμεν μόνον, ἐλεεινότεροι πάντων ἀνθρώπων ἐσμεν.

If we have hoped in Christ in this life only, we are the most to be pitied of all humans.

Here the inference Paul draws from the statement that the dead are not raised is not only that Christ has not been raised, but that our hope in Christ is necessarily only valid in our present life, and not after we die. The following paragraph continues to assert that Christ has been raised.

My purpose in going through these verses is to demonstrate the way representation is used to carry forward the argument about resurrection. Of course we can classify the protasis as 'first class' and 'determined as fulfilled', but that does not do justice to the whole burden of the argument, which is to show that the resurrection of the dead is true! Several of these clauses are presenting as fact statements with which Paul does not agree but *all have the same syntactic form*. The issue of the 'if' clauses being 'true' or 'untrue' is not part of the syntax, but forms part of the whole argument being put forward.

It is also the case that in Koine, as distinct from the classical language, the particle ἄρα might be added to the apodosis to strengthen the statement and affirm the conclusion. This does not occur in many examples in the NT, but we can see it here in verses 14, 15 and 18.[1]

Having set out a new approach, I will now go through examples from the four 'types' to offer an alternative analysis.

Type 1: Determined as Fulfilled

In the example below, the protasis in both sentences is identical, but context and biblical knowledge lead us to understand that the first protasis is non-factual. I have selected this example because it is cited by both Robertson and Wallace as a first-class condition; that is, one that is assumed to be 'true'. Wallace deals with this example by inserting 'assume to be true for argument's sake', but the truth of the proposition is not the issue. Wallace is right to

1. Other examples include Matthew 12:27, which is given here, but also the parallel passage in Luke 11:20, Galatians 2:21,3:29 and 5:11, as well as Hebrews 12:8.

show that the relation between the two clauses is what should concern us, but a clearer way to handle this is by treating the issue as what the Pharisees were saying of Jesus. Jesus picks up their comment and uses it to show that Satan cannot cast out Satan without his kingdom being divided.

Matthew 12:27

> καὶ εἰ ἐγὼ ἐν Βεελζεβοὺλ ἐκβάλλω τὰ δαιμόνια, οἱ υἱοι ὑμῶν ἐν τίνι ἐκβάλλουσιν;
> εἰ δὲ ἐν πνεύματι θεοῦ ἐγω ἐκβάλλω τὰ δαιμόνια, ἄρα ἔφθασεν ἐφ' ὑμᾶς ἡ βασιλεία τοῦ θεοῦ.
>
> If it is by Beelzebub I cast out demons, your sons: by whom do they cast out (demons)?
> But if by the spirit of God I cast out demons, then the kingdom of God has come on you.

These parallel sentences show clearly that the issue of 'real' versus 'unreal' or 'fact' versus 'counter fact' are not determined by syntax, since the protasis of both display the same verb form and conditional particle. The first protasis represents what Jesus' opponents were saying, but the second represents what Jesus was demonstrating by his healing actions. It is contextual and encyclopaedic information that informs us which of these is being presented as true. The apodosis in the first sentence is also enigmatic, giving rise to the inference that demons can only be cast out by a higher power. Since there were Jewish exorcists operating at that time, the question of their authenticity or power source is being brought to the fore. Focus on syntax alone will lead us into a cul-de-sac. Wallace has a section on 'assumption of truth' against 'truth', which is only necessary if syntactical criteria have been used to make unsupported pragmatic deductions such as the use of 'since' as a translation of 'if', which makes a nonsense of many clauses.

Type 2: Determined as Unfulfilled

In this category, the premise is *assumed to be contrary to fact.* The speaker does not believe – or is presenting himself as not believing – a particular situation is real. In Greek, the past tense of the indicative is used and this suggests that an event *might* have happened, but in fact did not. As we discussed above, the use of a subjunctive form in English has been the clue to this lack of belief in the statement, but younger English speakers seem to have lost the subjunctive verb forms almost entirely. When we hear *'If I was rich I would be able to buy a Porsche'*, we assume that the speaker is not in fact rich. The point of the statement is a relationship between income or wealth and the high cost of a particular car, rather than whether or not the speaker is rich. Of course, the truth of the protasis can only be determined by the context, but it is the relationship between the clauses that is the communicative thrust of the sentence. All we can say is that the speaker is *presenting* the protasis as non-factual.

In the NT, we can find examples of conditional sentences that seem to have the requisite grammatical form to fit this description but the protasis may, in the context, be true or at least vague. As before, the real issue is the relation between the two clauses of the condition and the belief of the one making the statement. This example from Luke 7:39 comes as a woman approaches Jesus to anoint him, after weeping over his feet and wiping them with her tears:

> οὗτος εἰ ἦν προφήτης, ἐγίνωσκεν ἂν τίς καὶ ποταπὴ ἡ γυνὴ ἥτις ἅπτεται αὐτοῦ, ὅτι ἁμαρτωλός ἐστιν.
>
> If this man were a prophet he would know what sort of woman touched him, that she is a sinner.

In this case, the Pharisee who was Jesus' host is doubting that Jesus was a prophet, but the issue is not the truth or otherwise of his belief but the relation of the protasis to the apodosis. In other words, prophets were expected to be able to discern the 'sin' or otherwise of those who approached them. Jesus turns the whole belief on its head by showing that he *did* recognise the woman's status, and beyond this he also brought out the Pharisee's lack of understanding of Jesus' own status. To put it simply, he *was* a prophet and he *did* know that she was a sinner, but by treating the protasis as a re-presentation of the thought of the Pharisee (did the latter voice his thought?), we have a more satisfactory understanding of this conditional sentence, and a better insight into the communicative intention of Luke. The use of the past tense in the Greek verbs may alert the reader to a proposition that the speaker does not believe, but the truth or otherwise is not determined by the syntax, but instead by context, as we have pointed out before.

On the other hand, in John 14:28, we have the grammatical form of an 'unreal' condition: namely, that Jesus was assuming that his disciples did not love him. There is no evidence to suggest this, and that makes 'unreal' inaccurate. The point is that since they love him they should rejoice:

> εἰ ἠγαπᾶτε με ἐχάρητε ἂν ὅτι πορεύομαι πρὸς τὸν πατέρα, ὅτι ὁ πατὴρ μείζων μού ἐστιν.
>
> If you loved me you would rejoice because I am going to the Father, because the Father is greater than I am.

I suggest that the communicative force of this particular conditional is to show the relationship between love for Jesus and willingness to allow him to return to the 'Father'.

The form may suggest that the protasis is being presented as untrue, but the context denies this. The earlier verses of the chapter focused strongly on the relationship between love and obedience, and it seems that it is better exegesis to use such a context to interpret this condition than to insist on a strict application of the 'unfulfilled' condition.

Type 3: Undetermined, But with Prospect of Determination

This is the category that has ἐάν with a subjunctive verb form in the protasis. Robertson has an elegant definition of the subject: 'the subjunctive mode brings the expectation within the horizon of a lively hope in spite of the cloud of hovering doubt'. As in indefinite clauses, vagueness rather than real uncertainty is the inference a reader is expected to draw from the use of this mode. One must always keep in mind the relationship between the protasis and the apodosis. This is the real point – not whether or not the protasis reflects actual fact.

John 19:12

> ἐὰν τοῦτον ἀπολύσῃς, οὐκ εἶ φίλος τοῦ Καίσαρος· πᾶς ὁ βασιλέα ἑαυτὸν ποιῶν ἀντιλέγει τῷ Καίσαρι.

If you release this man you are not a friend of Caesar. Everyone who makes himself a king is speaking against Caesar.

This protasis picks up the information that Pilate was 'seeking to release him'. It is the link between the two clauses, between releasing Jesus and maintaining a good relationship with Caesar, that raises the temperature. This link and the following explanatory utterance – 'everyone who makes himself a king speaks against Caesar' – stops Pilate from carrying out his original purpose, according to the writer of the Gospel. The presentation of Pilate's intention is then brought in to raise the argument about the potential threat that Jesus might pose to imperial rule. The issue is not whether or not the facts in either the protasis or apodosis are true, but how they were presented to Pilate.

Luke 22:67-68

εἰ σὺ εἶ ὁ Χριστός, εἰπὸν ἡμῖν. εἶπεν δὲ αὐτοῖς, Ἐὰν ὑμῖν εἴπω, οὐ μὴ πιστεύσητε· ἐὰν ἐρωτήσω, οὐ μὴ ἀποκριθῆτε.

'If you are the Christ, tell us.' He said to them, 'If I tell you, you will not believe; if I ask, you will not answer.'

In terms of the traditional analysis, the first protasis would be a 'class 1 condition'. The questioners did not believe it was true, but they were presenting it as a report of what others were saying of Jesus. In the second protasis – a Type 3 condition, undetermined but with prospect of determination – Jesus picks up their words and the anticipated outcome. Dancygier comments that what is being communicated in such sentences is the predictive link between the protasis and the apodosis.[1] As noted above, the subjunctive indicates vagueness rather than real uncertainty, but the context, as before, is the determining factor in deciding how uncertain the protasis is.

Mark 5:28 and Matthew 9:21

ἔλεγεν γὰρ ὅτι ἐὰν ἅψωμαι κἂν τῶν ἱματίων αὐτοῦ σωθήσομαι.

For she said 'If I touch even his clothes I will be healed.'

1. Dancygier, B. (1998) *Conditionals and Prediction.* Cambridge: CUP, p. 72.

ἔλεγεν γὰρ ἐν ἑαυτῇ· ἐὰν μόνον ἅψωμαι τοῦ ἱματίου αὐτοῦ σωθήσομαι.

For she said to herself 'If I only touch his cloak I will be healed.'

Wallace rather unfortunately suggests that there must have been considerable doubt in the woman's mind – presumably based on the grammatical form of the condition, but that is a totally gratuitous assumption. The shocking act of a woman touching a Jewish rabbi, and a woman whose touch would render the rabbi ceremonially unclean at that, does not support serious doubt in the mind of the woman in this incident. There are so many protases of this type which exegetes accept as merely indefinite but very likely to be fulfilled, that it is unfortunate that form is making the running in interpretation here.[1] As always, it is the relationship between the clauses that should be the focus.

Type 4: Remote Prospect of Determination

There are few conditionals in this category and they are very close to the indirect questions noted below. But there are several examples in Acts where a treatment by re-presentation is a more perspicacious way of analysing the Greek. I note one example in narrative and one within material presented as speech.

Acts 27:39

ὅτε δὲ ἡμέρα ἐγένετο, τὴν γῆν οὐκ ἐπεγίνωσκον, κόλπον δέ τινα κατενόουν ἔξοντα αἰγιαλὸν εἰς ὃν ἐβουλεύοντο εἰ δύναιντο ἐξῶσαι τὸ πλοῖον.

When it became daylight, they did not recognise the country, but they spotted a bay which had a beach on which they planned to get the boat to land if they were able.

The inference that we may reasonably draw from this verse is that the crew indicated that they planned to beach the ship in the bay 'if they were able' (εἰ δύναιντο). The following account shows that although the attempt was made it was not successful, and the ship was broken up by the waves. The verb ἐβουλεύοντο ('they were planning') clearly implies a proposition that was made

1. For example, see John 14:3.

manifest to those present, and demonstrates not only a protasis, but also an apodosis, which is a re-presentation.

In Acts 24:19 there is another example, but the apodosis is not a complete clause, although the meaning is clear:

> τινὲς δὲ ἀπὸ τῆς Ἀσίας Ἰουδαῖοι, οὓς ἔδει ἐπὶ σοῦ παρεῖναι καὶ κατηγορεῖν εἴ τι ἔχοιεν πρὸς ἐμέ.
>
> But some Judeans from Asia, who should have been present before you to accuse (me) also if they had anything to say against me.

Here it seems that Paul did not believe that these men from Asia had anything substantial to say against him, and he is claiming that if they had any accusation to make they should have been present.

Moulton does not consider this category to be present in the NT, seeing the examples as 'indirect questions', and he may be correct.[1] When the issue is dealt with as re-presentation, then we have no problem. This leads us onto the examples of indirect questions in predominantly Lucan material, and the obvious link as introducing a re-presentation.

Εἰ to Introduce an Indirect Question

This use of the conditional particle is very pertinent to this argument, since an indirect question is very obviously a case of re-presentation of something said by another. The following example makes this clear.

Mark 15:44

> ὁ δὲ Πιλᾶτος ἐθαύμασεν εἰ ἤδη τέθνηκεν καὶ προσκαλεσάμενος τὸν κεντυρίωνα ἐπηρώτησεν αὔτον εἰ πάλαι ἀπέθανεν.
>
> Pilate wondered if he was already dead and, summoning the centurion, asked him if he had already died.

Here we have two questions from Pilate: 'Is he already dead?' and 'Has he died?' Both are introduced by the conditional particle.

---

1. Moulton, J.H. (1908) *A Grammar of NT Greek: Prolegomena.* Edinburgh: T. & T. Clark, p. 196.

Acts 25:20

> ἀπορούμενος δὲ ἐγὼ τὴν περὶ τούτων ζήτησιν ἔλεγον εἰ βούλοιτο πορεύεσθαι εἰς Ἱεροσόλυμα κἀκεῖ κρίνεσθαι περὶ τούτων.
>
> Being at a loss about the inquiry (I should present) about these matters, I asked him if he were willing to go to Jerusalem and there be judged concerning these matters.

Here the governor Festus is narrating what he said to Paul when inquiring whether or not he wanted to go back to Jerusalem to be tried: *Are you willing to go to Jerusalem to be judged about these matters?*

These examples show that although the particle εἰ appears in the protasis of each, it introduces a question, rather than a supposition to be followed by a conclusion.

Examples from Discourses of Epictetus

Examples from this philosopher tend to be rather long and difficult to isolate from their context, but I will give several below to support my hypothesis, and to give further evidence that it is the relationship of both clauses which is the speaker's point.

1.9.1

> Εἰ ταῦτα ἐστιν ἀληθῆ τὰ περὶ τῆς συγγενείας τοῦ θεοῦ καὶ ἀνθρώπων λεγόμενα ὑπὸ τῶν φιλοσόφων, τί ἄλλο ἀπολείπεται τοῖς ἀνθρώποις ἢ τὸ τοῦ Σωκράτους, μηδέποτε πρὸς τὸν πυθόμενον ποδαπός ἐστιν εἰπεῖν ὅτι 'Αθηναῖος ἢ Κορίνθος, ἀλλ' ὅτι κόσμιος;
>
> If these things are true which are said about the common family of God and men by philosophers, what else is left for men other than the position of Socrates, never to say to an enquirer 'I am Athenian' or 'I am Corinthian' but 'I am (a citizen) of the world.'

This would be a Type 1 condition in a traditional analysis, with present tense in both clauses. If the protasis is true, then the apodosis follows as a conclusion. The protasis is putting forward a position as true for the sake of argument, and it is clearly a re-presentation of 'what is said'. The heading for this section of argument is 'us being related to God', and it is this belief that is being re-presented here.

2.18.1

> ἂν θέλῃς ἀναγνωστικὸς εἶναι, ἀναγίγνωσκε·ἂν γραφικός, γράφε.
>
> If you wish to be a reader, read; if (you wish to be) a scribe, write.

As stated above, the issue is the potentiality of the protasis, not whether or not it is a fact. The apodosis gives an instruction based on the likelihood of the protasis being a fact. Epictetus is beginning his argument about making progress in the philosophical life by giving examples of how progress is made in any sphere of activity. The second clause is interesting because of the ellipsis of both the main verb and the infinitive.

In his *Verbal Aspect*, Stanley Porter introduced different categories to those quoted above from Robertson but again acknowledged that in non-biblical Greek, as well as biblical Greek, these categories were in fact mixed.[1] His examples and assertions regarding tense use are expansive, and I cannot do them justice in this short chapter, but they come up against the same problem: we cannot decide the grounds on which a speaker or writer chose a particular construction, and the decision regarding whether or not a clause contains an 'assertion according to fact' or 'contrary to fact' will not be decided on syntactic grounds.

Porter explains the difficult use of tense forms in certain examples by claiming that it is an aspectual choice which has caused the writer or speaker to use certain tenses. This may well be true, but, since we are not easily able to understand such choice in every case, we are still left with pragmatic decisions based on context. Porter, like Wallace, does focus on the type of relationship between the protasis and the apodosis, but, again,

---

1. Porter, S.E. (1989) *Verbal Aspect in the Greek of the New Testament*. New York: Peter Lang, pp. 291-320. His classification includes verb tenses, and differs slightly from that of Robertson, with the nomenclature being as follows: Assertion, Assertion to the contrary, Projection and Expectation.

presenting a taxonomy of potential relationships such as cause and effect, or ground and inference, does not help to determine relationships outside of the context in which the utterance occurs. In fact, he acknowledges:

> The conditional is a construction that functions in the realm of pragmatic usage, linking two smaller units within one larger discourse unit.

In this, we can agree.

Conclusion

This chapter has attempted to chart a new path through the forest of competing accounts of conditional sentences in Greek. It is generally agreed by those who support syntactic criteria for 'defining' types of condition that in the NT these types are frequently mixed. Some identification depends on verb tense, and yet there are several examples of conditional sentences, such as the example from Epictetus above, in which no verb occurs.[1] Since these syntactic criteria alone *cannot* tell us about the truth or falsehood of a protasis, or even about whether or not the speaker believes what he states to be the case for the sake of argument, then we must acknowledge the input of pragmatics from which we are able to make these deductions. By viewing the protasis as a representation of a position held by the speaker or some other, we are closer to understanding the purpose of such a protasis in his wider argument and the communicative intention of the author.

1. Romans 8:17.

Chapter 7
Summing-Up and Loose Ends

This book was conceived as an introduction to the use of relevance theory by biblical scholars. Since the theory looks at the interpretation of text from the perspective of the communicative intention of the putative author, it allows readers to examine old problems from a new angle. One of the strongest claims of the theory is that humans, by producing utterances, have the intention to communicate, a claim that is important when considered from a literary background in which deconstruction has reigned supreme. Relevance theory also provides a theoretical underpinning for human strategies of communication and, in addition, for the miscommunication that frequently occurs.

The rigour employed in biblical studies in researching historical context, provenance, and authorial or editorial identity marries well with the need for the encyclopaedic and contextual information that is a prerequisite for successful communication, and which is an essential part of relevance theory. The theory also leads an exegete to examine the reasons for the interpretative and perhaps intuitive decisions he has made from the perspective of both the 'original' reader and the reader from a later time who lacks such information. It is generally acknowledged that we all come to a text with presuppositions, and that many of these are unrecognised – far less acknowledged. Such presuppositions then become part of the contextual information which we bring to the text but of which we are unaware. The need to spell out implicatures is an important part of an individual's preparation for good exegesis, but for those who are very familiar with the biblical text it may seem to be an unnecessary distraction.

A new generation of biblical students will look at the text without such a background, but in turn they will bring their own presuppositions that may have led them to misunderstand the context or world view of the participants in the biblical documents. In short, we need to examine how relevance drives communication and gives the exegete a new tool for investigating an old text.

In particular, we need to recognise that the literalness which we have taken as 'normal' is not, in fact, the default option. Not only do we use 'loose resemblance' all the time in everyday speech, but also literalness is not the default option in the biblical text itself. Perhaps it is hard to accept that a sacred text is less – or really more – than literal. The discipline of rhetoric in the ancient world made use of tropes to achieve extra effects, and assumed that 'utterances come with a presumption of literalness'.[1] The concept of literalness is 'analytically useful', but cannot be taken to be normative. We have become so accustomed to the use of figurative language that we are no longer aware of its ubiquitous presence.

Time and Tense

One fact that has become more apparent to me over the years I have studied and applied this theory is that humans *do* use relevance to interpret utterances in normal life, but revert to grammatical props to determine meaning in a biblical text. This is nowhere more apparent than in the ongoing dispute over the importance of aspect versus tense in the identifying of time in Greek verbs. Decisions are made on an 'aspectual' basis, but this frequently turns out to be a pragmatic decision based on what 'makes sense'. In essence, tense selection is part of authorial choice, but we cannot always recover the reason for such a selection, nor identify the particular 'aspect' that the writer had in mind. Yes, it is an aspectual choice but 2,000 years later we may not be able to confidently state *why* he had a perfective or imperfective aspect in mind.

It is always good to take account of what a Greek says about his own language, and the comments of Basil Mandilaras on the language of the non-literary papyri are infinitely useful:

1. Wilson and Sperber (2012) p. 86.

> Aspect depends not only on the use of the particular tense, but also on the meaning of the particular verb involved. Sometimes, too, adverbial expressions in the sentence point to a differentiation of aspect, which tense alone could not determine definitely.[1]

This is so obviously important but so little considered in this whole debate, which has been extremely acrimonious in the past. By the time of Koine, many verbs, particularly in NT texts, only display certain tenses in their non-indicative forms. As Mandilaras notes, some verbs have a meaning that predisposes their use of a particular tense form. Non-indicative tense forms are limited, and so time cannot be decided on tense alone, but from interaction with the whole sentence. One small example from Matthew 2:8 shows this:

> πέμψας αὐτοὺς εἰς Βηθλέεμ εἶπεν, Πορευθέντες ἐξετάσατε ἀκριβῶς, περὶ τοῦ παιδίου·
>
> Sending them to Bethlehem he said, 'Go and search carefully about the child.'

Although the aorist tense has been used for the participle 'sending', pragmatic inference tells us that he could not have sent them *before* he spoke. Sometimes adverbs are added to make a time reference clear, as in John 9:25:

> ἓν οἶδα ὅτι τυφλὸς ὢν ἄρτι βλέπω
>
> I know one thing, that although I was blind I now see.

The adverb ἄρτι guides the reader to read the participle as having reference to an earlier state. It seems that although we employ pragmatic inference, we crave the security of a grammatical form to affirm such an inference. In conclusion, it is pragmatic inferencing guided by relevance that in fact determines how we identify and read temporal reference. The application of relevance theory to this hot topic of tense and aspect needs much more careful work, but I have included it here in end notes to open the way for further study.

Finally, I hope that biblical scholars will be encouraged to use this cognitive and communicative approach which modern

1. Mandilaras (1973) p. 54.

linguistics has been dialoguing with for almost thirty years now. There is always a fear in biblical studies that linguistic theories will confuse and diminish the traditional approaches, which may be why scholars in the field have used an eclectic approach to linguistic studies, rather than adopting any one model. There is nothing to fear and everything to be gained from at least considering those insights that help to deal with difficult passages and 'hard' sayings. This is relevant!

Glossary

Adversative
Introducing a contrast.

Apodosis
The concluding clause in a conditional sentence; completing a sentence containing an 'if' clause, and usually expressing a result concomitant on the reality of the conditional clause (protasis).

Bridging assumptions
The presuppositions necessary to make a statement relevant; in John 2:3 the phrase 'when the wine ran out' requires the bridging assumption that wine was a recognised part of a wedding celebration.

Chiasmus
In Greek it means two crossed lines and was a well known literary feature; in the Greek of John 1:1 'the Word was with God and God was the Word' is a chiasm, but in English we reverse the order to show that 'the Word' is the subject of the second part of the sentence.

Classical Greek
This is usually taken to refer to the language used by the great dramatists and orators of sixth to fourth century Athens. It was probably never the language of conversation; that might be found in some of the characters in the plays of Aristophanes.

Cognition
The mental processes that accompany interpretation.

Concessive
Usually introduced by 'although' or 'even if', it allows a situation that is contrary to expectation.

Diatribe

A feature of rhetoric in Classical Greek and down to post-New Testament era, it presents the arguments of an opponent and then proceeds to demolish them. Verbal irony is a common feature of this type of argumentation.

Dissonance

Features of text that seem to contradict earlier statements or presentations.

Echoic

A term used in relevance theory to describe the representation of words used earlier but also indicating the attitude of the new speaker.

Ellipsis

This refers to missing words which have to be supplied from earlier text or speech.

Explicatures

These are 'propositions which are explicitly communicated.' (Chrystal, 2008.)

Implicatures

Extra information that a reader or hear may infer from text or speech given, but that is not essential to make sense of that given text or speech. It will give a richer understanding, but the responsibility for inference rests with the hearer or reader.

Koine Greek

This term is used to describe the speech of the Greek world and beyond from the time of Alexander the Great until after New Testament times, third century BCE until third or fourth century CE. It is often divided into 'literary' and 'non-literary', and is the language in which the New Testament was written.

Optative

This is a grammatical 'mood' or verb form which was a feature of Classical Greek, but became much less frequent and, although found in the New Testament, is far from common. It expresses a distant or potential state of affairs and is used mostly for indirect questions.

Ostensive

This is a relevance theory term used to express the intention of a speaker to communicate something.

Pagan Greek

This is a term used by biblical scholars to refer to Greek text that is not part of the Greek Old Testament, New Testament or early Christian writings.

Participial clause

This is a grammatical term that refers to a string of speech which contains a participle, in English usually a verb part ending in '-ing'.

Pericope

A discrete piece of text; in reference to the biblical material it is often used of a story, incident or section of teaching.

Pragmatics

Usually used to refer to the study of language as it is used, that is in context. Chrystal's definition: 'General pragmatics is the study of the principles governing the communicative use of language, especially as encountered in conversations.'

Pronomial

This refers to the use of pronouns such as I, you, he, she, it and they.

Protasis

This is the 'if' clause of a conditional sentence.

Relevance theory

There are two principles of relevance which Dan Sperber and Deirdre Wilson lay out:

1. Human cognition tends to be geared to the maximisation of relevance;
2. Every act of ostensive communication communicates a presumption of its own optimal relevance. [Sperber, D. and Wilson, D. (1995) *Relevance*. Cambridge: Blackwell, p. 260.]

Their theory of communication is based on these two principles. Chrystal: 'A theory of communication and cognition which claims that human cognition is geared to the maximizing of relevance.'

Re-presentation

The repetition of, or reference to, something already said or written. It may be acknowledged by quotation marks but frequently occurs informally with no acknowledgement. Indeed, speakers or writers are not always aware of the fact that it has been written or spoken already.

Resumptive

A continuing reference to something said before, often a pronoun.

Syntax

Modern term for 'grammar', or how language works in terms of the rules or combination of parts of speech.

Telic

Used by older biblical scholars to indicate purpose or intention, but modern linguists use it in discussions of verbal aspect.

Underdetermined

A meaning that is not stated but assumed; may refer to multiple meanings for one word. We can say that the word 'grace' is underdetermined in English because it has a wide range of reference. In Greek, participles are underdetermined because they have hidden logical relations within them such as time, concession, cause etc.

Bibliography

Ancient Texts

Arrian, Flavius. *Epictetus, The Discourses.* Loeb Classical Library. Harvard University Press. 1998 reprint.

Polybius. *The Histories.* Loeb Classical Library. Harvard University Press. 2010 reprint.

Thucydides. *History of the Peloponnesian War.* Loeb Classical Library 108. Harvard University Press. 1919.

Xenophon. *Anabasis.* Loeb Classical Library. London: Heinemann. 1921 & 1932.

Modern Texts

Abbott, E.A. (1906) *Johannine Grammar.* London: A. & C. Black.

Almazan Garcia, E.M. (2002) *Intertextuality and Translation: A Relevance-Theoretic Approach.* M.Phil. Dissertation, University of Salford.

Barclay, J.G. (1987) 'Mirror-reading a polemical letter: Galatians as a test case', *JSNT* 31.73-93.

Barclay, J.M.G. (2015) *Paul and the Gift.* GR, Michigan: Eerdmans.

Barnett, P. (1997) *The Second Epistle to the Corinthians.* NICNT. GR, Michigan: Eerdmans.

Barrett, C.K. (1968) *The First Epistle to the Corinthians.* Peabody, Massachusetts: Hendrickson, 1987.

——. (1973) *The Second Epistle to the Corinthians.* BNTC. London: Black.

——. (1978) *The Gospel According to St John.* Philadelphia: Westminster.

——. (1994 and 1998) *A Critical and Exegetical Commentary on the Acts of the Apostles.* 2 vols. Edinburgh: T. & T. Clark.

Betz, H.D. (1985) *2 Corinthians 8 and 9.* Philadelphia: Fortress Press.

Blakemore, D. (1992) *Understanding Utterances.* Oxford: Blackwell.

——. (2002) *Relevance and Linguistic Meaning.* Cambridge: Cambridge University Press.

Blass, F., and Debrunner, A. (1961) *A Greek Grammar of the NT and Other Early Christian Literature*, trans. R.W. Funk. Chicago: University of Chicago Press.

Bruce, F.F. (1971) *1 and 2 Corinthians.* London: Oliphants.

——. (1976 reprint) *Acts of the Apostles.* Leicester: Inter-Varsity Press.

Buth, R. (1992) 'οὖν and asyndeton in John's Gospel' in Black, D.A. (ed.) *Linguistics and New Testament Interpretation.* Nashville: Broadman.

Campbell, D.A. (2009) *The Deliverance of God: An Apocalyptic Rereading of Justification in Paul.* GR, Michigan: Eerdmans.

Caragounis, C.C. (2004) *The Development of Greek and the New Testament.* Tübingen: Mohr Siebeck.

Carston, R. and Uchida, S. (1998) *Relevance Theory: Applications and Implications.* Amsterdam: John Benjamins.

Carston, R. (2002) *Thoughts and Utterances.* Oxford: Blackwell.

Chapman, S. and Routledge, C. (2009) *Key Ideas in Linguistics and the Philosophy of Language.* Edinburgh: Edinburgh University Press.

Chrystal, D. (2008) *A Dictionary of Linguistics and Phonetics.* 6th ed. Oxford: Blackwell.

Clark, B. (2013) *Relevance Theory.* Cambridge: Cambridge University Press.

Dancygier, B. (1998) *Conditionals and Prediction.* Cambridge: Cambridge University Press.

Dunn, J.D.G. (1988) *Romans 9-16.* WBC. Nashville: Thomas Nelson.

Ehrensberger, K. (2008) 'Paul and the authority of Scripture' in Porter, S.E. and Stanley, C.D. (eds.) *As It Is Written: Studying Paul's Use of Scripture.* pp. 291-319. Atlanta: SBL.

Evans, C. (1989) *To See and not Perceive: Isaiah 6:9-10 in Early Jewish and Christian Interpretation.* JSOTSup 64. Sheffield: JSOT.

Fee, G. (1987) *The First Epistle to the Corinthians.* GR, Michigan: Eerdmans.

Fitzmyer, J.A. (2008) *First Corinthians.* London: Yale University Press.

Furnish, V.P. (1984) *II Corinthians.* Anchor Bible 32A: New York.

Garland, D.E. (2003) *1 Corinthians.* GR, Michigan: Baker.

Gutt, E-A. (2004) 'Quotation and translation as higher-order acts of communication'. Unpublished paper.

Haenchen, E. (1971) *The Acts of the Apostles.* Oxford: Blackwell.

Hays, R.B. (1989) *Echoes of Scripture in the Letters of Paul.* New Haven: Yale University Press.

Hollenbach, B. (1983) 'Lest they should turn again and be forgiven' in *Bible Translator* 34 pp. 312-321.

Hooker, M. (1991) *The Gospel According to St Mark.* London: A. & C. Black.

Horsley, R.A. (1998) *Corinthians.* Nashville: Abingdon.

Hughes, P.E. (1962) *Second Epistle to the Corinthians.* GR, Michigan: Eerdmans.

Ifantidou, E. (2001) *Evidentials and Relevance.* Amsterdam: John Benjamins.

Jack, A. (1999) *Texts Reading Texts, Sacred and Secular.* JSNT 179. Sheffield: Sheffield Academic Press.

Jannaris, A.N. (1897) *An Historical Greek Grammar.* London: MacMillan.

Levinsohn, S. (2000) *Discourse Features of New Testament Greek.* Dallas: SIL.

Mackenzie, I. (2002) *Paradigms of Reading.* Basingstoke: Palgrave Macmillan.

Mandilaras, B. (1973) *The Verb in the Greek Non-literary Papyri.* Athens: Hellenic Ministry of Culture and Sciences.

Marcus, J. (1984) 'Mark 4:10-12 and Marcan Epistemology'. *JBL* 103, 557-74.

——. (2000) *Mark 1-8.* AB. New York: Doubleday.

Morris, L. (1984) *The Gospel According to John.* GR, Michigan: Eerdmans. Reprint.

Moule, C.F.D. (1969) 'Mark 4:1-20 Yet Once More' in *Neotestamentica et Semitica: Studies in Honour of Matthew Black* eds. E.E. Ellis and M.E. Wilcox. Edinburgh: T. & T. Clark.

Moulton, J.H. (1908) *A Grammar of New Testament Greek: Prologomena.* Edinburgh: T. & T. Clark.

Moyise, S. (2008) *Evoking Scripture.* London: T. & T. Clark.

Nanos, M. (2002) *The Irony of Galatians.* Minneapolis: Fortress.

Noh, E-J. (2000) *Metarepresentation: A Relevance-Theoretic Approach.* Amsterdam: John Benjamins.

Nolland, J. (1989) *Luke.* WBC 35A. Dallas: Word.

Peppiatt, L. (2015) *Women and Worship at Corinth.* Eugene, Oregon: Wipf & Stock.

Porter, S.E. (1989) *Verbal Aspect in the Greek of the New Testament.* New York: Peter Lang.

——. (1992) *Idioms of the Greek New Testament.* Sheffield: Sheffield Academic Press.

——. (2008) 'Allusions and Echoes' in Porter, S.E. and Stanley, C.D. (eds.) *As It Is Written: Studying Paul's Use of Scripture.* pp. 29-40. Atlanta: SBL.

Porter, S.E. and Stanley, C.D. (eds.) (2008) *As It Is Written: Studying Paul's Use of Scripture.* Atlanta: SBL.

Räisänen, H. (1990) *The Messianic Secret in Mark's Gospel.* SNTW. Edinburgh: T. & T. Clark.

Robertson, A.T. (1934) *A Grammar of the Greek NT in the Light of Historical Research.* 4th edition. Nashville: Broadman.

Sacks, J. (2009) *Covenant and Conversation. Genesis: the Book of Beginnings.* New Milford/London/Jerusalem: Maggid, Koren.

Schnackenburg, R. (1982) *The Gospel According to St John.* Vols. 1-3. New York: Crossroads.

Seow, C.L. (2013) *Job 1-21: Interpretation and Commentary.* GR, Michigan: Eerdmans.

Sim, M.G. (2004) 'Under determinacy in Greek Participles' in *Bible Translator* 55, pp. 348-359.

——. (2011) *Marking Thought and Talk in New Testament Greek.* Cambridge: James Clarke & Co.

——. (2011) 'καίπερ as a constraint on relevance' in *Festschrift for Stephen Levinsohn.* Logos Biblical Software.

——. (2014) 'The Genitive Absolute in Discourse: More Than a Change of Subject' in Reflections on Lexicography. *Perspectives on Linguistics and Ancient Languages* 4. Piscataway, NJ: Gorgias Press.

Sperber, D. (1994) 'Understanding verbal understanding' in Khalfa, J. (ed.) *What is Intelligence?* pp. 179-198. Cambridge: Cambridge University Press.

—— (ed.). (2000) *Metarepresentations: A Multidisciplinary Perspective.* Oxford: Oxford University Press.

Sperber, D. and Wilson, D. (1986/1995) *Relevance: Communication and Cognition.* Oxford: Blackwell.

Stanley, C.D. *Arguing with Scripture.* New York: T. & T. Clark.

—— (ed.). (2012) *Paul and Scripture.* Atlanta: SBL.

Taylor, V. (1981 reprint) *The Gospel According to St Mark.* GR, Michigan: Baker.

Theissen, G. (1982) *The Social Setting of Pauline Christianity.* Edinburgh: T. & T. Clark.

Thistleton, A.C. (2000) *The First Epistle to the Corinthians: A Commentary on the Greek Text.* GR, Michigan: Eerdmans.

Turner, N. (1963) *A Grammar of New Testament Greek* III. *Syntax.* Edinburgh: T. & T. Clark.

Thrall, M. (2004) *2 Corinthians 1-7.* 2nd edition. London: T. & T. Clark.

——. (2004) *2 Corinthians 8-13.* 2nd edition. London: T. & T. Clark.

Uchida, S. (1998) 'Text and Relevance' in Carston, R. and Uchida, S. (eds.) *Relevance Theory: Applications and Implications.* Amsterdam: John Benjamins.

Wallace, D.B. (1996) *Greek Grammar Beyond the Basics.* Grand Rapids: Zondervan.

Watson, F. (1985) 'The Social Function of Mark's Secrecy Theme', JSNT 24:49-69.

Wilson, D. (2011) 'Relevance and the interpretation of literary works', UCL Working Papers in Linguistics.

Wilson, D. and Sperber, D. (2012) *Meaning and Relevance.* Cambridge: Cambridge University Press.

Witherington III, B. (1995) *Conflict and Community in Corinth.* GR, Michigan: Eerdmans.

Wright, N.T. (1986) 'ἁρπαγμός and the meaning of Philippians 2:5-11', *JTS* 37: 321-52.

Wright, T. (2011) *New Testament for Everyone.* London: SPCK.

Suggestions for Further Reading

I have selected some recent works which should be of particular value to biblical scholars. The standard text books by Sperber and Wilson, published in 1986 and 1995, although a hugely important resource, have been largely superseded in recent years.

The most recent and readable introductory text is Billy Clark's *Relevance Theory*, published in 2013 by Cambridge University Press. It is designed for different audiences: those with no knowledge of relevance theory, those with some knowledge and others who have already worked on the theory. Students familiar with the theory will find the latter part of the book most interesting but for all it is a lucid and engaging account of the theory with many examples and also exercises for those who want to test their comprehension of what has been discussed.

Another early book is Diane Blakemore's *Understanding Utterance*, published by Blackwell in 1992. It is described as 'An introduction to Pragmatics' and is totally non-threatening and readily comprehensible.

For those who were interested in the fifth chapter of this book, and in discourse studies in general, Diane Blakemore's later book *Relevance and Linguistic Meaning*, published in 2002 by Cambridge University Press, will be extremely useful.

The issue of underdeterminacy is dealt with in Robyn Carston's *Thoughts and Utterances*, published in 2002 by Blackwell. This is heavier going for non-linguists but gives a scholarly and readable presentation of explicit and implicit communication.

Finally, those who wish to work further on the issue of how humans metarepresent one another will find Eun-Ju Noh's *Metarepresentation* well worth reading (published by John Benjamins in 2000).

More General Helpful Works

David Chrystal's *A Dictionary of Linguistics and Phonetics*, published by Blackwell, has been an invaluable volume for many students, as has *Key Ideas in Linguistics and the Philosophy of Language*, edited by Siobhan Chapman and Christopher Routledge and published by Edinburgh University Press in 2009.

Index of Scripture References and Other Ancient Literature

John *(continued)*

Acts

Romans

1 Corinthians

2 Corinthians

Galatians

Philippians

1 Thessalonians

2 Thessalonians

Hebrews

1 Peter

Index of Subjects and Authors

You may also be interested in

Marking Thought and Talk in New Testament Greek

New Light from Linguistics on the Particles ἵνα *and* ὅτι

Margaret G. Sim

Print ISBN: 978 0 227 17377 0
PDF ISBN: 978 0 227 90328 5

Aimed at both biblical scholars and those interested in linguistic theory, this book makes use of insights from a modern theory of communication, relevance theory, in examining the function of the particle ἵνα in New Testament Greek.

Challenging accepted wisdom, Margaret Sim claims that the particle does not have a lexical meaning of 'in order that', but that it alerts the reader to expect an interpretation of the thought or attitude of the implied speaker or author. Evidence is adduced from pagan Greek and in particular the writings of Polybius, Dionysius of Halicarnassus, and Epictetus, as well as the New Testament. The implications of this claim open up opportunities for fresh interpretation of many problematic texts.

Available now with more excellent titles in Paperback, Hardback, PDF and Epub formats from James Clarke & Co

www.jamesclarke.co

www.ingramcontent.com/pod-product-compliance
Lightning Source LLC
LaVergne TN
LVHW020633100826
845148LV00012B/2177
9781532603679